travel

THE STONES OF ITALY

AGENTS

AMERICA . THE MACMILLAN COMPANY
        60 FIFTH AVENUE, NEW YORK
AUSTRALASIA THE OXFORD UNIVERSITY PRESS
        205 FLINDERS LANE, MELBOURNE
CANADA . . THE MACMILLAN COMPANY OF CANADA, LTD.
        ST. MARTIN'S HOUSE, 70 BOND STREET, TORONTO, 2
INDIA . . MACMILLAN & COMPANY, LTD.
        276 HORNBY ROAD, BOMBAY
        294 BOW BAZAR STREET, CALCUTTA
        NORTH BEACH ROAD, MADRAS

CONTENTS

LIST OF ILLUSTRATIONS

Sketch Map of Italy on page xvi

INTRODUCTION

A GREAT English poet once wrote,

> Open my heart and you will see
> Graved inside of it, "Italy"!

Nor was Browning alone in his adoration. Shakespeare, Byron, Shelley and Keats among poets, Reynolds, Watts, Leighton and Burne-Jones among artists, besides numerous other talented men of ancient and modern times, have been unanimous in their praise. Some through the medium of the pen, others no less eloquently with the brush, have given unstinted testimony to the beauty of that land, which, from its infancy, has ever taken a high place in the arts of peace no less than in the arts of war.

A journey to the Eternal City, even for those who spoke the tongue of Homer, was the *ne plus ultra* of their aspirations. Certainly they had no need to go to other countries in search of refinement. "Roma Caput Mundi", a familiar expression in olden days, was undoubtedly apposite. Like the expressions "See Naples and die", "Venice, Queen of the Adriatic", "Bononia Alma Mater Studiorum", and many another, it bears powerful testimony to the extraordinary attraction of the land of the Latin race.

The exhilarating qualities of the air, the melodious language of the inhabitants and their temperament, differing from that of all other countries, are features appealing to a great many people. But undoubtedly the *colour* of Italy—the colour of its mountains, its skies, its sea, and, above all, the mellowed stones of its ancient monuments—is a dominant factor in its fascination.

Colour is light, and light is colour. As the flowers of the earth absorb the colour in the rays of the sun, so these ancient stones have retained something of the mellow glory of the sunlight of ages. Light, or colour, is Life, and is the most essential of all elements. In fact when a world of the Universe has lost its own light, or that projected upon it by some kindly sun, such a world has passed for ever into absolute oblivion.

Christ, as we know, called Himself " The Light of the World ", and stated that unless we looked through Him we should not see. He did not say, " I am the Sound ", " I am the Electricity ", " I am the Steam " ; but most emphatically, " I am the Light ". Great masters like Giorgione, Veronese, Tintoretto or Titian would probably have been ignored for ever had they been born under some grey sky of the North. The origin of the strength, the essential beauty of the early Italian schools of painting is bound up with the acknowledgement of inexplicable phenomena, the most important of which is undoubtedly light.

Colour appeals to all, but more especially to those who are born under a brilliant sun; and to Italians its appeal is inherent. Rich and poor, young and old, the lady in her palace no less than the woman in the fields, but particularly the artist, all have an intense longing for colour. Before everything else it was the beautiful golden hair, the blue eyes and the rosy cheeks of the English boys brought before Pope Gregory, that caused his amazed exclamation, " These are not Angles, but Angels ". And yet those lads were doubtless comely in other ways. Their sweetness of manner, their gentleness of voice struck the Pope far less than the flaxen hair and clear complexion which appealed to him. A beautiful fresco painting of the sixteenth century at St. Gregory in Rome gives us a good idea of the lovely colour of those three English boys.

In the realm of Light, as in the realm of Nature, there are many degrees of beauty which appeal to us according to our temperament and our environment. Take for instance the deep, almost conventional blue of the Egyptian sky. It is beautiful, grand, immeasurable in its depth—as immeasurable as the span of the dynasties of that ancient land. It is deep, vast, but unquestionably too blue ; and one could call it almost theatrical, because it is unsoftened by the atmosphere. It makes all form and shadow, by contrast, as hard as if cut with a knife. On the other hand, the English sky and mist add *too much* mystery to distant objects, and therefore make the background too suddenly indefinite in comparison with the foreground.

If we study the subject with care we come to the conclusion that the beautiful sky of Italy, so blue and yet so transparent, is the happy medium.

The wonders of Nature are illimitable ; but poetry and art being the handiwork of man, he alone, with his songs, his pictures, his sculpture, his religion, has exalted the beauty of Nature to an ideal by adding to it his poetic imagination.

Some years ago I visited the Grand Cañon of Arizona—one of the great wonders of the world. I had heard so much of it while in America that I made it a point of duty not to return to Europe without seeing the world-renowned chasms of that region. This resolution was taken more especially because I had heard so much of the splendid colour, and I wished to compare its beauty with that of other countries.

I went there with an old friend of mine, Commendatore Colasanti, General Director of Fine Arts of Italy, and one of the most distinguished art critics of our age. I took with me the necessary materials for painting, in order that I might carry away, if not a picture, at least an impression of the colour. After a long journey from Los Angeles we arrived at the Grand Cañon. It runs through a plateau many thousands of feet above sea-level, in a most fantastic way, for hundreds of miles, carrying its waters towards the Mexican Gulf.

What immensity ! What colour ! I remained breathless. It seemed to me almost as if I had been transported to one of those horrible passes among the mountains, so wonderfully described in Dante's *Inferno* ; that one, for example, where he saw the frightful whirlwind of lost souls, in which he recognised Paolo and Francesca, the sight of whom made him fall " as a dead body falls ".

Such a fantastic background would have appealed to Wagner as a magnificent setting for one of his operas. It reminded me somewhat of that which may have been in the first days of Creation—of that indescribable period of chaos, when the waters, receding, cut their irresistible way through the mountains, carving deep in the primordial rocks their tortuous courses between frowning precipices —an epoch of terrestrial convulsion too awful to conceive.

At some points the cañon is about one mile wide, and the actual run of water, which to-day is reduced to the width of an ordinary river, is so deep down that it is almost beyond the range of vision. One may gain some idea of its depth from the fact that it takes nearly four hours to descend by mule to the bottom of the fissure, in some places 6000 feet deep.

And yet, in spite of its terrible vastness, and wonderful peacock-coloured rocks, I was left, some-how, more frightened than charmed. And why? Because of the conventionality of the colour—even more conventional than that of the Swiss mountains —and because of its total want of poetry or association with the history of man.

No nymphs, no naiads, no fauns could be expected to arise from those waters. No Venus fair as that of the Capitol or sublime as that of Milo could be pictured testing the temperature of the stream with her alabaster feet. Nor could the pools, by any stretch of the imagination, be called, as the Romans called the enchanting lake of Nemi, " Diana's

STONES OF ITALY

CHAPTER I

THE ALPS

To make a memorable entry into Italy and enjoy what may well be said to be one of the greatest and most impressive views that man can conceive, one should not go by the ordinary route, Paris—Modane—Turin. That is the way of the commonplace tourist, who goes to Italy and boasts of having " done it " in two weeks, and Rome from top to bottom in three days. No doubt that is the cheaper and more comfortable way—the one that appeals to the mind of the ordinary business man who can only be absent from his bank or government office for a week or two.

No. I intend to go to Italy in the good company of two friends of taste, culture and refinement ; not necessarily with a graduate of Oxford or Cambridge, but with one who would stop more readily at a glorious sunset than at a football match, a golf final or a boat race. I want companions who rejoice in reading the message of an ancient stone, a century-old oak, or a bronze perhaps buried for centuries

beneath the crystalline waters of Lake Nemi. With
such as try to realise more and more what beauty
means, who are ever seeking for some elevating
thought, I intend making a solemn entry into
Italy. Together we will feel, if possible, a little of
what souls like Hannibal and Napoleon should
have felt when, on reaching the summit of the Alps,
they saw below, as in a stupendous dream, the
enchanted land of Italia—the land where even
the birds seem to sing in the language of Dante or
Manzoni. With the latter we, too, may sing :

> Ovunque il guardo io giro
> Immenso Iddio ti veggo
> Nelle opere tue ti ammiro
> E ti riconosco in me.

With such friends as I have described, I organised
this unconventional tour and detrained at Modane,
leaving the coaches full of passengers who, in
twenty-five minutes, would be in Italy without
knowing how. Outside the station we took the
motor-bus going up Mont Cenis. The automobile,
not always very comfortable, follows the river which,
springing from the very summit of the Alps, runs
down towards Modane at a terrible speed, turning
to the right and to the left, now dropping suddenly
into a ravine, now forming a lake, elsewhere eating
into the rocks, the arches of bridges or the corners
of mill-buildings which the intrepid mountain-
dweller has built across the torrent to grind corn

for his daily bread. At every turn of the steep road there is a surprise waiting for us. Fresh villages come into view and others disappear ; new peaks, new visions, new dreams of beauty and colour. The air becomes lighter and lighter, we feel as if we want to shout aloud, to laugh, to kiss the very earth.

After several hours of continuous climbing we reach a certain plateau which is the highest point in the road. From here begins the descent into Italy, and from here a wonderful view opens out before our eyes—a view of which no fervent imagination, no pen, no brush could give you the faintest idea. You remain without breath and you wonder why you have let so many years of your life pass without making a supreme effort to drink sooner of the beauties of this celestial vision.

If the air is so exhilarating, the infinitely gradu- ated blues of the atmosphere and the mountains are even more so. With its cobalt you find Prussian blue, rose madder, yellow cadmium, and if you look still more closely you end by finding the whole palette of Titian or Veronese. No pyramids, no Temple of Solomon, no other monuments of ancient or modern times, could bring you so close to the Creator and the supernatural as that un- forgettable view.

What a wonderful gift of God is that given to some men, to be able to admire such expressions of His greatness ! A man who remains indifferent before a panoramic view of this description, may well be called a corpse, a stone, or a human marionette—a figure only moving if somebody else operates a string. Such an one is almost as insensible as the millstone which crushes, crushes, until it is worn out with crushing, and does not know why or for whom it labours.

A sunset or a moonlight effect upon those heights no one should attempt to describe. Both add marvellous mystery to the panorama, and both reveal still more than does the daylight, the severity of line or contour of the mountains. The profile of a mountain is as the profile of a woman. Both may be beautiful or both may be commonplace. That of the Italian Alps is so great in severity that one could define it as Etruscan; while that of the Swiss mountains with its commonplace, monotonous peaks might be compared to an enormous saw.

At the great height we have now reached there is a most comfortable hotel where we may spend the night and wait for another glorious vision, the sunrise over Mont Cenis. A small lake stretches before us, marking the highest level the road attains. The waters of this lake are so deeply blue that they may be compared to a colossal slab of *lapis lazuli*. This strong blue note in the foreground of the picture seems to render still more refined the blue of the surrounding mountain.

It was most probably on this very plateau, or on some similar height of the Alps, that Hannibal, at the head of his formidable army, nearly twenty centuries ago, looked down with fiery eye upon that Italy which, in order not to break an oath made to his dying father, Hamilcar, he had at all costs to invade and humiliate. With such an army at his back and at so tremendous a height, much nearer to heaven than those down in the valleys, one could almost excuse him for feeling sure of victory. But destiny had decreed that the wild African should not desecrate Rome, the Empress of the World, with his barbarian foot. None of his elephants, and few of his savage legions, lived to return to their country. What a sight must have been the crossing of the Alps by this stupendous army !

Napoleon, in imitating Hannibal, had better luck. Crossing the mountains without great loss he reached Milan. Here, in the Duomo, impatiently snatching the crown from the hands of the Pope, he crowned himself. He passed some ineffectual years in Italy, but eventually, like Hannibal, he had to recross the Alps and leave La Bella Italia to her own destiny.

It is here on this platform, once trodden perhaps by the two greatest fanatics of the world, whose hearts were not in the least softened in the presence of an all but supernatural spectacle of beauty, that we breathe for the first time the mild and invigorating Italian air. We stand beneath a sun that most probably will not cease to shine

over us throughout our artistic pilgrimage round
Italy.

We are now at the frontier. We show our pass-
ports. We give a last look at the French gendarmes,
and for the first time we pass under the protection of
the Italian gendarmes—the *carabinieri Reali d'Italia.*

I was at luncheon with Sir Edward Burne-Jones
not long before his death and, talking about his
beautiful mosaics in the American church in Rome,
I asked him if he was satisfied with the way in
which his cartoons had been carried out. To my
great amazement he told me he had never seen
the mosaics, because he had never been to Italy
again since the Mont Cenis tunnel had been
opened. Before that there had been across the
Alps a regular *diligence* service by which he had
travelled, and he did not like to spoil the sublime
recollection of those days. He was quite right.
Only one who has crossed the Alps as Burne-Jones
did—and as we did—can realise fully the meaning
of his determination.

From this natural frontier we began to descend
by a most tortuous road, enjoying magnificent
views of the great green valley below, where
Susa's brown walls, with the arch of Augustus,
Roman gate, old castle, grey slate roofs and high
church towers lie sheltered from the winds that
meet us.

The descent from Mont Cenis is still more
striking than the ascent from Modane. We follow

the way taken by Napoleon, though at that time the going must have been very different. New panoramas lie before our eyes, new valleys, new mountain slopes all covered with tiny vineyards and charming little villages of wooden houses with big balconies, each well protected by its heavy slate roof.

Not an inch of ground is neglected. On the sides of the mountains, wherever it is possible to rest a foot, we see terraces, each a miniature orchard or vineyard, producing its fruit or wine of quality.

It is here that you begin to understand and appreciate the industry and strength of purpose of the Italian nation. With slabs of rock split from their own hillsides they build their homes, their factories and their hazardous bridges, and pave their tortuous roads. On the earth-terraces, they cultivate their vegetables, while with the abundant water which they call *carbon bianco* (white coal) they produce the greatest energy-power mankind has ever known—electricity. In the bowels of those mountains is hydraulic power enough to substitute for all the motive energy that Europe now derives from coal and oil. In fact Italy of to-day has the greatest hydraulic plant in Europe, and soon that power will be transmitted to the very end of the Italian peninsula. When that time comes, not one single ton of foreign coal will ever again be imported into Italy. The cold waters of the Alps will smelt the hard steel in the furnaces !

The gigantic pipes of the electric works, descending from enormous heights, where they harness the power of torrents and waterfalls, are much diminished by distance, appearing as mere threads of cotton running down the mountain slopes. They accompany us almost down to the valley, and in themselves are enough to give us an idea of the future prospects of Italy.

It is no exaggeration to say that from Modane down to Spezia you will not see a piece of black coal. Everything is moved by the other, much cleaner and hotter fuel—electricity.

Near Susa we again take the train and in less than two hours we see Superga, the mausoleum of the Kings of Italy, which rises at the very gates of Turin. This town we reach by a picturesque way amongst large vineyards and mulberry trees, whose leaves are utilised to feed myriads of those worms which patiently spin the silk used to adorn both the elegant figures of ladies and the consecrated shoulders of bishops all over the world.

CHAPTER II

TURIN

WE are in Turin, the first important town on the way to Rome. No better title ever could have been given to this town than that of " The Cradle of Modern Italy ". In fact, it was not only the birthplace of many princes and kings of the illustrious family of Savoy, but for many years it was also the first capital of Modern Italy, the birthplace of the first Italian parliament.

On our arrival we do not need to be told that we are in a royal town. We know it instinctively. The magnificence of the streets, the spaciousness of the squares, the nobility of the monuments, the majesty of the innumerable palaces, the grandeur of the churches and the castle, are more than sufficient to tell the visitor that he is in a town of great moment—a town of kings.

At a very remote period Turin was the capital of the Taurini, from whom was derived the name of Augusta Taurinorum and, later on, Turin.

On his way towards Rome, in 218 B.C., Hannibal

left part of his army at Turin ; this occupation
lasted only a few years, as, after his futile enterprise in the Italian peninsula, Hannibal had to
surrender Turin with all the other provinces he
had subjugated, bringing back with him only the
gratification of having seen Rome from Tivoli,
near which town he settled with his barbarous
hordes at a spot called even to this day " Hannibal's
Camps ".

Turin lies on a perfectly level plain among hills
irrigated by one of the most picturesque rivers in
Italy, the Po, a river which merely touches the
town at some points, and elsewhere cuts right
through it. Near the Castello del Valentino it
offers a most beautiful vista, especially at a point
opposite the castle, where the reflection of the latter
may be seen in its clear waters. Great poplar
trees fringe the banks of the river on both sides for
many miles.

This city, with its many monuments, palaces
and churches, has for a background on the north
side the entire range of majestic peaks, thousands
of feet in altitude and running from Tenda to
Monte Rosa to form a stupendous amphitheatre of
various tones of blue. One might spend hours in
contemplating so splendid a panorama, especially
at sunrise or sunset ; it would be difficult to say
which of the two experiences would be more
impressive.

In the evening when the sun is getting near

the horizon, all the great and luxuriant valley of the Po, some thousands of square miles in extent, is enveloped in a cold vapourous shadow. Only the innumerable peaks of the mountains remain burning like volcanoes against the dark blue sky. The rosy, flaming tints and cold shadows cast by one peak beyond another leave ever-haunting memories of these exquisitely contoured mountains.

If a sunset is grand, even more splendid perhaps is a sunrise. While Turin is still asleep, and the silence of the valley is only broken by the first songs of the birds, a gold glare appears behind the Alps to tell us of the arrival of another glorious day. The solemnity of these moments can only be compared with that of a total eclipse, though it is without any of those shiverings and uncanny sensations which always accompany the latter phenomenon. A gentle breeze begins to rise, the golden glare behind the mountains increases with every second, and very soon all the summits, the Superga and the Mole Antonelliana—seeming almost as high as the Alps—receive the first golden kisses of the sun. Little by little that misty mantle that covers the valley begins to disperse, and there stands out in the principal square of the town the great equestrian statue of Emmanuel Philiberto, a mighty king-warrior sheathing his sword after conquest. He emerges from the gentle mist like the great phantom of a sentinel who has watched faithfully over the town all night, and now puts away his sword as if all danger were over. This masterpiece is by the hand of Marocchetti, the celebrated Italian sculptor who also created the beautiful equestrian statue of Cœur de Lion in Old Palace Yard, Westminster. Many are the monuments of that city, as we have said, but the most important are the Castello del Valentino, Porta Palatina, Palazzo Carignano and Palazzo Madama. The many churches of various periods are built of brick and stone, and have acquired a pale brown tone very characteristic of the town. Undoubtedly the finest of all these is the Cathedral, dating from the year 1496, with an isolated campanile and a most unique chapel behind the High Altar. This chapel was built entirely in polished grey marble by the House of Savoy, and in the centre in a special sanctuary of similar stone, is a precious relic—perhaps the greatest relic of Christianity—the sacred Shroud in which our Lord was buried. It was brought to Italy by St. Helena, mother of Constantine, and it still shows the impression of the body of Christ. The chapel is placed at the back of the Altar, and is reached by long flights of steps on either side. Everything around speaks of the veneration and preciousness of the contents. The shrine is opened with great pomp at very long intervals of time before the King of Italy, who holds the key.

The church of the Servites in the Piazza Emmanuel Philiberto, and the other opposite it, are beautiful monuments of the seventeenth century. The Freius monument, though not beautiful, is interesting because it is a reminder of the great work of the Mont Cenis tunnel, which cost Italy and France so many millions and so many lives.

This stupendous undertaking, started in 1857, was completed in 1871 at the cost of £3,000,000. The tunnel is seven and a half miles long, and the middle reaches an altitude of 4246 feet above the sea. It was considered one of the greatest engineering works of the world at the time of its completion. It was started about the same time by the Italians on the one side and by the French on the other. After many years of toil the two parties came so near that one could hear the hammers of the other. There was great consternation when these sounds were heard coming from one side and not from ahead, as should have been the case. It was only a misleading acoustic phenomenon, for the direction of both branches was perfect. When the parties met great rejoicing took place, not only there in the bowels of the earth but also throughout Italy, France and the whole of Europe, for the great commercial value of the tunnel was acknowledged from the first.

It is most fascinating to enter Italy by the Mont Cenis Pass, but such a pleasure can only be enjoyed at the proper season. Splendid as are the views at this time, unforgettable would be a journey over these heights in bad weather. As a matter of fact the Pass is, in winter, totally blocked with snow.

The first hospice on Mont Cenis was founded by monks as far back as the ninth century, and ever since it has proved one of the most philanthropic institutions in the world.

It seems that Turin has always been a prominent contributor to Italy's prosperity. From 1860 to 1865 it was the capital town. To-day it is the commercial capital of the Italian motor industry. A glance from the train as one passes close to the enormous factory of the Fiat Company is sufficient indication of Turin's supremacy in this direction. In no other city have I seen a manufactory that can boast of such a building. It should be sufficient to say that on the very top of this skyscraper, as the Americans would call it, a great motor-track is laid down to test the speed of cars before they leave the works. To watch a car running at sixty or seventy miles an hour on the roof of a building is not a normal experience. Italy to-day exports cars all over the world, and is already a formidable competitor in the world's motor-market.

The many marble tablets affixed to the walls of houses in the town tell us that in Turin were born and bred men like Massimo D'Azelio, Cavour and many other celebrated writers, politicians, generals and scientists of past times. It is not surprising that the best talent of Italy should have

THE SIDE DOOR OF THE CATHEDRAL OF S. LORENZO, GENOA

they are not in keeping with the rest of the façade. From an artistic point of view Genoa might well be termed the town of palaces and *portoni*. These doorways are always open, and through them we pass to the courtyards, also of great architectural importance. That of the Academy of Fine Arts perhaps surpasses them all, and among the best are those of the Palazzo del Municipio, the Ducal Palace, the Palazzi Doria and Durazzo and Brignole, the last with an exquisite gallery inside.

Genoa is also rich in other artistic treasures. S. Carignano, a miniature reproduction of St. Peter's, beautifully situated on an eminence, and S. Siro, the first Christian church built in Genoa, are the two most important of the minor churches of the town. The cathedral of S. Lorenzo, of the ninth century, is a notable monument, both in size and style. We went over it time and again, admiring its beautiful details.

The side door, illustrated here, is an excellent example of the architectural detail of the church, even more beautiful at the present day than when it was first built, owing to the colourful hand of time. The colouring of those carvings, the columns, the little Gothic window, as well as the warmth of the wall on the left, make it characteristic of the Stones of old Genoa.

One of our first visits was to the house of Christopher Columbus, with the historic Porta Sovrana beyond and its frowning bastions on either hand. The little house (which I painted upon the spot, surrounded by a crowd of appreciative youngsters) was for years the dwelling where the discoverer toiled with his father.

It is not certain whether he was living there when he conceived the great idea of searching for another world, or finding a new passage to the East. At the time he lived there he must have been very poor. As his father went about his trade of wool-comber he little imagined that this humble house of his would, centuries later, be visited and gazed at almost as a sanctuary by every visitor to the town.

The sea never saw a more gentle-hearted or more intrepid sailor than Columbus. Not even Cabot from Bristol or Vasco da Gama from Lisbon ventured so far into the unknown, or pursued discovery under such difficulties as he overcame. And then, what a fate! After so many perils, and such faith in his theory which gave birth to the era of the New World, he was brought back to Spain in chains like a malefactor, while the land he had discovered after so much anxiety was called by the name of another — Amerigo Vespucci. Such is the ingratitude of men!

Another point of great interest in the same picture is the great pointed arch in the middle distance. This was once the main gate of the city and those flanking bastions tell us how strongly it had to be guarded.

As a warning of its power, Genoa for many years hung in festoons upon that gate, as a trophy of war, the chains taken from the port of Pisa. Even after the uniting of Italy, the chains remained hanging there ; but the day came when Genoa magnanimously gave them back to Pisa, who received them with the greatest jubilation. To-day you may see them in the Campo Santo there amongst the artistic and historic relics of that town.

Porta Sovrana, with Columbus's house and the adjoining dwellings, exemplifies well the richness of colouring pervading the whole town.

A view of the port from one of the many heights of the town will give a fair idea of its great size and commercial importance. From the numerous money-changers' establishments we may gather that much foreign money comes into the town from all parts of the world. Such was its wealth in the past that Genoa was considered as the " Bank of Europe ". Many European states, particularly Spain, borrowed money from Genoa.

Little by little, however, it lost all its foreign possessions. Corsica was the last to go, being ceded to France so late as 1763. Had the island been kept, Napoleon would have remained an Italian, and most probably a different map of Europe would have been the consequence.

In our wanderings we shall notice a great number of charitable institutions, of which the old

Ospedal del Pannuantone is the most remarkable.
It was built in 1439.

We also notice the opera-house Carlo Felice, so
splendidly decorated inside that Covent Garden
would appear in comparison a mere warehouse.

The Palace of the University is imposing and
the Staglione cemetery is without doubt one of the
sights of Europe. It is not so much a cemetery as
a great open-air sculpture gallery. Of course among
the many beautiful marble monuments there are
some that are not the best that Italy can produce.
Two facts stand out forcibly : the reverence for
the dead, indeed almost amounting to a cult, and
the great love of the masses for sculptural art.

On our way to Carrara, which we desired to see
because of its world-renowned marble quarries,
we went through no less than ninety-eight tunnels !
Nearly all the way the line is cut through the
mountain sides, descending sheer to the sea. It is
a long journey, relieved by a constant succession
of the most surprising scenic effects that can be
imagined.

Santa Margherita, Rapallo, Portofino, Sestri
Levante, and scores of other little villages, one by
one appeared before our eyes as we emerged from
those dark tunnels. Some of them are washed by
the waves, others stand upon rocky islets, some
much higher on the slopes from which twisted
flights of steps descend perhaps to miniature bays
with white sands washed by transparent waters.

PORTA SOVRANO, WITH THE HOUSE OF CHRISTOPHER COLUMBUS,
GENOA (page 21)

Still others are only to be approached by winding roads cut into the living rock. Each vista is made more charming by orange and lemon groves, oleanders, rhododendrons and pine trees, the aroma of which can be scented even as we rush by in the train.

The brilliant colours of the houses, some painted yellow, some red, some white, provide bright relief from the grey ferruginous rocks. These and the blue sky and sea—clear as a mirror near the shore— are all things which keep one for ever at the window of the train in wonder. There you may realise, better even than in the Alps, the meaning of the familiar expression, " Il bel sole d'Italia ".

At last we come to the final tunnel and soon after we stop for a good cup of coffee at Spezia, and the naval base of Italy—where the greater warships of the Italian navy have been launched.

After Spezia we see rising from the waters the contour of the Isola del Ferro, whose extraordinary magnetism often upsets the compasses of ships that pass near by. An hour or two later our attention is called to the opposite side of the railway line, for we are running parallel to the range of the great Carrara mountains, so grand in colour and so marvellous in their outlines. The enormous size of these mountains makes all nearby buildings look almost like toy houses with miniature gardens.

CHAPTER IV

CARRARA

How very few people realise the fact that every white marble step, pavement or fireplace in our homes or offices, every white cross in our cemeteries, every bit of marble statuary, ancient or modern, had to be quarried from those high mountains of Carrara. So it is, so it has ever been, and so it will be to the end of time, for, with the exception of some creamish-white marble from Greece, there is no other white marble in the world. This fact alone is enough to explain the enormous marble trade of Carrara.

The approach is noticeable for many miles before the town is reached. Everywhere there is marble where common stone would be used elsewhere. Front door steps of the poorest houses, cornices, balconies, pavements,—all are marble.

Carrara stands on the slopes of the colossal ranges of white mountains running parallel to the Mediterranean, and only three or four miles distant from the sea.

RAVACCIONE QUARRIES, CARRARA

The day following our arrival we visited some of the more important quarries, which we reached only after a tortuous and long journey on a narrow-gauge railway. The train goes up with empty trucks and comes down laden with great blocks of all shapes and sizes to supply the needs of the whole world.

Each truck has its men at the brakes ready to answer the signal of the engine-man. At each turn of the way we enjoyed grand views, and when we reached the highest station the panorama was beautiful beyond description.

It is to termini such as that we reached, high up in the mountains, that all the " streams " of marble blocks converge, to be finally carted away down to the embarking places. The descent, therefore, of each block from the actual quarry is accomplished partly on sledges and partly by train. In the picture here reproduced will be seen one of those thousands of streams converging upon one of the railheads.

Up among these immensities one is confused. The feeling is due chiefly to the glare of the sun on the extensive fields of marble, glistening white like snow. At intervals there is heard the melancholy sound of the horn announcing the imminent explosion of a mine. At this sound everyone seeks refuge, and a few minutes later a deafening roar is heard echoing and re-echoing from crag to crag. When the last reverberation has died away

4

one seems to be plunged again into the profound silence of the infinite.

The second time we ascended these heights a large mine was fired. They had been working at it for many weeks. On the crest of a mountain a scaffold had been erected in several stages, and through this was an enormous pole furnished with a large chisel at the point. This was lifted and dropped every few seconds with terrific force by a gang of men on each stage.

When the hole so formed was deep enough, about a hundred feet, corrosive acid was dropped in and a large chamber formed at the bottom of the hole. This was then charged with dynamite and eventually fired by electricity. The explosion was announced days before by printed notices everywhere.

The moment came and, with all the workers of the surrounding mines watching, it was fired. The mountain was split open with a deafening report, the sun was eclipsed by the dust and débris, and the outline of the mountain range became unrecognisable.

But the Roman method of quarrying was, naturally, quite different. Holes were bored in the marble and into them wooden poles were driven with much force. Then water was poured upon the timber and allowed to sink in. In swelling, the wood burst the marble at the required place. Even to-day traces of this method can be noticed on the sides of abandoned quarries.

Sculptors of all ages and countries have gone to Carrara to select their blocks—Michael Angelo and Canova among them. Sargent in more recent times went there to paint. I did likewise, but only with the object of providing comparison between the immaculate whiteness of those clean surfaces and the brush-work of a greater artist, Time.

The beautiful cathedral in Carrara gives us a good idea of what time has done to its marbles, once white as that in the quarries near by.

In the employment of marbles it seems as if England was next in importance to Rome and Athens. The great number of important English firms that have been established at Carrara for many years testifies to the enormous development of marble decoration in these islands. Walton, Goddy and Cripps, and the Anselm Company, are two of the oldest firms, and carry on an ever-increasing trade with England.

CHAPTER V

ROME AND ITS SURROUNDINGS

WE leave Carrara and our eyes are greatly relieved, for the constant glare of white marble is really blinding. No wonder that in so small a place there are to be found so many oculists ready to provide one with any description of spectacles.

We spend the night in the train and by the brilliant moonlight we see, as we pass, villages large and small, some perched picturesquely upon rocks like crows' nests. But we only stop at Pisa and Leghorn. We skirt the pine forest of San Rossore, and early in the morning we stop at the old port Civita Vecchia. The deep blue of the sea is ever with you here, every now and again scattered by groups of rocks or small hills crowned with pine-woods whose characteristic appearance and refined tone of green is one of the features of the Roman Campagna.

On the left you are accompanied by a line of hills and immense plains of pasture land where are to be seen flocks of sheep and herds of oxen with exceptionally fine and lengthy horns. They stand watching in long lines, stupefied at the rushing of the train as it travels Romewards.

The sun begins to show itself. It seems to burst forth with an immense cargo of gold-dust which is spilled everywhere, bathing with its gold and giving life to everything it touches. The larks are singing, the dew shines on every leaf, Nature is waking to another glorious day. Palo, one of the nearest seaside resorts to modern Rome, and then Ladispoli are left behind, and in about an hour's time every passenger rushes to the window as some enthusiastic young member of an English family exclaims, " Mother, Mother, the Tiber ! " It is true. We are coasting the yellow Tiber, which, like an enormous snake, glides among the hayfields of the Campagna in great silence and dignity. It comes from the Eternal City, runs past Ostia, the old Roman port, and thence into the blue Mediterranean.

Yes ! it is the Tiber—the most historic river in the world. It is the river that witnessed the birth and growth of the greatest of all empires ever built by man. The river that for century upon century divided the land of the Latins from the Etruscan lands and that, with the persistence of Nature, battered and corroded the stones of the bridges that first united those two great races who founded the civilisation of the world.

We travel quickly, almost in a semicircle round

the city ; and cross the river at the point where, after its long and winding course, it bursts through the ancient walls of Rome into the classic Campagna. We do not wish to miss a stone, or a tree, and much less the blue Alban hills on the right. So we keep passing from one side of the carriage to the other until another exclamation bursts from every tongue, " St. Peter's ! St. Peter's ! " The enormous dome, exquisitely proportioned, representing one of the greatest conceptions of human genius, appears as an immense symbol dominating the material things of earth even as it does the things of the spirit. It gives greeting—Rome's first greeting—to all, rich and poor, pagan no less than Christian.

A few minutes later the train stops before a perfectly ordered line of porters, who shout in all imaginable keys, " *Signori si cambia* " (All change !). They take our luggage, and with an inexpressible sensation in our hearts we place our reverent feet upon the stones of the Eternal City.

After a good breakfast at a comfortable hotel, we start upon our artistic pilgrimage.

To get well acquainted with our surroundings we determine not to stop at any of the usual show-places, the museums or monuments. Instead we arrange merely to go about in a very comfortable motor without stopping except for luncheon. This we had planned to take at that most frequented restaurant in the Forum Traiano, the Ulpia, where you may enjoy an exquisite dish of macaroni and

an excellent flask of Castelli Romani wine amongst
the old brick walls of what was once a famous
basilica built by Apollodorus. What ironic fate !
That a magnificent temple built by the celebrated
architect from Damascus, should be turned into
a restaurant !

The reader has already been given to understand that these pages on the Stones of Italy are
not intended to give anything like a continuous
story of the rise or decadence of Roman power.
They purport to be merely a record of impressions
culled from the various interlacing periods of art,
ancient and modern. He must not therefore be
surprised if he finds us in spite of our great respect
and love for everything that is old and beautiful,
jumping with the ease of an acrobat from the cold
stones of the Forum to a warm *piatto di maccheroni*.
The comparatively limited time we could spend
amongst the stones of the different towns, and the
time I permitted myself for recording with my
brush, would allow of no different method.

The thrill that took possession of us at our first
glimpse of the dome of St. Peter's seen from the
train never abated during the several weeks we
spent in Rome. Rather it increased as time went
on. The long familiarity I had with the city,
although I had not visited it for many years,
enabled us to see many things that others could
scarcely have seen in a much longer period.

In spite of what we may call our revolutionary

archæological outlook, we preferred to revel first amongst the stones of classic Rome, the Rome of the Kings, the Republic and the Empire ; then to pass to Rome of the Church, to which our own times are so strongly linked. Consequently we spent our first week in the Forum or the Palatine Hill, in the Palace of the Cæsars, the Colosseum and its surroundings.

In almost every description of Rome the reader is placed with his shoulder to the Porta del Popolo, and there he is told to look at the big Piazza of that name with its Egyptian obelisk. Then there are pointed out the three streets, Babuino, Corso and Ripetta, that spread fanwise before him.

But if you wish for a really profound impression of the majesty and greatness of Rome, you should go almost with the eyes shut to the very top of the Victor Emmanuel monument and then open them. From this height you feel as if you were upon the very pivot of Rome. Beneath your feet you see the great Forum with its mutilated columns, steps, colossal pillars, triumphal arches, the Palace of the Caesars, the Colosseum, the Tiber, the Pantheon, St. Peter's, all Rome in fact and the glorious Campagna around it. And all this scene of splendour seems to be crowned by a continuous line or background of historic hills with only one gap therein, that for which old Tiber makes on leaving the walls of Rome.

The buildings, both public and private, being

THE ARCH OF SEPTIMUS SEVERUS, ROME (page 35)

built principally of Travertine, give a " tone "
which is very uncommon. A brown intermingled
with all gradations of yellow may be said to be the
prevailing and characteristic colour of the city. It
is difficult to express the appearance of grandeur
it has in contrast with the clear blue sky above.

CHAPTER VI

ROME : THE FORUM

AFTER a long time, during which a species of fervent contemplation filled us with deep amazement, we descended to the Forum, which lies on the further side of the Capitol Hill. The Tabularium, or sacred place where were kept the laws of Rome engraved upon hard stones (and on the site of which, centuries after, was built the central palace of the Capitol), divides the Capitol of Michael Angelo from the Forum. On the slope of the hill, at the very foot of that massive structure, starts the famous Via Sacra, all paved with stones. On the left we have the Temple of the Twelve Gods, the other of Vespasian, the Basilica Opinia and the Temple of Concord : on the right the Temple of Saturn.

Soon after the Via Sacra branches into two, one branch passing near the arch of Septimus Severus and by the remains of the Duilian columns, the other between the great Basilica Giulia and the Forum, erected by and named after Julius Caesar.

The column of Phocas, the eight Honorary Bases, the plinths of the Marcus Aurelius monument, with beautiful high relief representations of sacrificial beasts, are the most conspicuous remains. Near the last named stood the equestrian statue of that Emperor, now in the Piazza Campidoglio.

We approach the Forum by the way which passes under the fine arch of Septimus Severus, now the more impressive by reason of the colouring of ages, as seen in the plate near this page, and come upon the greatest of all relics of ancient Rome—the tomb of Romulus.

From ancient writings, it had been fairly well determined where the famous Lapis Nigra, or Black Slab, should have been located. But no one had ever dreamed that it would be found so little below the present level of the Forum. The fear of upsetting other precious monuments made researches the more difficult, but one day, not many years ago, between the joinings of some marble slabs was noticed a dark stone below. With frantic excitement the overlying slabs were removed, and to the joy of all present, and later of all the learned world, there came to light the long-sought Lapis Nigra. It was the Black Slab that covered the mortal remains of Romulus, the founder of Rome. No other archæological discovery ever caused so great a sensation.

Like a series of geological strata you see in the Forum the indication of its various ages of construction. It would seem as if at one time the level was much below the present, and that subsequently it had to be raised on account of the infiltration of the waters of the Tiber.

The great wooden beams, buried much below the present floor, which were brought to light only a few years ago, show the level of the original foundations. At the time when this important discovery was made a man engaged upon the excavations, seeing how interested I was in his task, threw me a small piece of that wood : I brought it over here to England—a " fossil " of the Mistress of the World ! It will not be out of place to remind the reader that England, above all other foreign countries, took an interest in these excavations.

The base and steps of the column of Phocas, the latter presumably surmounted by the statue of that Emperor, were excavated at the expense of the Countess of Devonshire in 1816. Most probably Byron touched the heart of the Countess with his lines in " Childe Harold " :

> Tully was not so eloquent as thou,
> Thou nameless column with the buried base.

Had such an enlightened spirit of respect and admiration been evinced in the past, many more ancient remains would doubtless have been spared destruction. Pope Gregory intervened to a certain extent, but it was the great Pius IX. who, in a most practical way, finally put a stop to the destroying of previous relics of art. An important part, however, was taken by the activities of several Englishmen in creating reverence and love for the things of the past. Chief among these was undoubtedly Lord Elgin although, of course, his activities were unconnected with Rome.

It was due to his example, chiefly manifested in his rescue of the priceless Phidian marbles, now in the British Museum, that many other classical remains have been preserved. Else surely they would have gone the way of those remains that have been incorporated in the foundations of newer buildings or used as paving stones.

From the Lapis Nigra we follow the paved road of the Forum and meet again the Via Sacra, closely surrounded by the monumental remains of an age of incomparable greatness and artistic superiority.

At the corner of the Basilica Giulia we are confronted with the remains of the Temple of Castor and Pollux, consisting principally of three magnificent Corinthian columns. Attached to the last of the Honorary Bases we note the little shrine of Venus, where the Via Sacra turns towards the Arch of Titus, passing round the temple and tomb of Caesar. Very little is left of the latter, but from Cassius and Suetonius we may gather the great importance of the structure : " The Triumvirs likewise built a tomb to Julius Caesar in the middle

of the Forum with a hostel that was to be for ever
inviolable. Before the temple was erected a monolithic column of Numidian marble, twenty feet
high, inscribed ' To the Father of His Country '.
At the time of the death of Nero the temple of
Caesar was struck by lightning, the heads of all the
statues fell off simultaneously and Augustus' sceptre
was dashed from his hand.

" Undoubtedly this occurrence aroused the super-
stitions of the Romans and from it was foretold the
fall of the Roman Empire. Very near to this was
the spot, according to Livy, where Virginius in
order to save his beautiful daughter from dis-
honour, snatched a butcher's knife and plunged it
into her heart before the judge. Dionisius beautifully pictures the sympathy of the assembly: ' The
relatives of the virgin increased still more the discontent of the Romans by carrying her bier into
the Forum with her body all adorned in great
splendours; bringing it through the principal and
most conspicuous streets of the town. All the
matrons and young girls came out of their houses
lamenting her loss. Some dropped flowers upon
her corpse and others their girdles or veils, some
their children's toys, while others even cut off their
curls and placed them upon the bier. Many men
purchased ornaments from neighbouring shops, or
received them gratis from the shopkeepers, that
they might contribute to the pomp by the best
presents they could, proper to the occasion. In

such manner was the funeral celebrated all through the city.' "

In front of Caesar's temple must once have been the Curtian lake, or fire-pit as it was often called. It is said that a fanatical warrior, Marcus Curtius, in order to pacify the gods, leaped into the lake mounted and in full uniform and was never seen again. From some remains of pumice found on that spot many believe that at one time there must have been here some sort of volcanic spout from which smoke and fire may have issued.

Near to Caesar's temple also stood the Temple of Vesta, erected by Numa in A.U.C. 37. " It was made round as a symbol of the earth ", Ovid tells us, and according to Pliny it was covered with bronze of Syracuse. Here with great care was preserved the Palladium, the Holy Fire, which was kept burning day and night by six vestals who made solemn vows for thirty years, the breaking of which was punishable by burial alive.

Facing this spot, on the other side of the Via Sacra, are the eight majestic Corinthian columns of the Temple of Antoninus and Faustina. They are monoliths of Cipollino, a beautifully figured white and green marble from Greece.

From where we stand by Caesar's tomb the ground begins to rise to a considerable height, and the slope is thickly built with palaces, terraces and temples, all grouped in an impressive but casual fashion. This is the approach to the famous

Palatine Hill, the chief interest of which is its Palace of the Caesars.

It was on the top of this most historic hill that Romulus and his soldiers laid the first stones of the Roma Quadrada, which in the course of centuries was enlarged until it sheltered as many as six million inhabitants.

Remains of the Arcadian, the Kingly, the Republican and the Imperial periods are all to be found here on this hill, rendering the spot intensely fascinating to the archæologist and the historian no less than to the ordinary visitor.

After Romulus had freed himself from his brother Remus and settled permanently upon the Palatine Hill with his legion, he might well have exclaimed, " Hic manebimus optime " (" Here we shall remain most comfortably "). In fact there they planted their standards, raised their tents, and there they laid the first stone of what later was to be the Empire of the World. How proud they would have been if they could have looked into the future and seen that, even many centuries after its fall, kings, emperors, and the intellect of the whole world would tread those stones and pay reverence to the greatness of that Empire. Like the British Empire of to-day it brought the benefits of civilisation to every corner of the known world.

With the Palace of the Caesars on the right and the three large arches of the Basilica of Constantine

THE COLISEUM, ROME (page 45)

usually called Temple of Peace on the left, ascending all the time, we come to the highest point of the Via Sacra, the Clivus Palatinus. Just here the Via Sacra becomes the Clivus Triumphalis, and it passes under the Arch of Titus. It then descends towards the Arch of Constantine and the Colosseum.

Little is left of the old Arch of Titus ; but from what remains we can gather some idea of the height to which art attained under that Emperor. On two large marble panels in high relief still in place under the arch we may see the triumphant Titus in his chariot, with his soldiers carrying the table of the Shewbread and the seven-branched golden candlesticks taken from the Temple of Jerusalem.

It is a grand example of art. No wonder that it has always been considered the apogee of high-relief sculpture produced by old Rome. High-relief has ever been much in vogue amongst Roman artists. Even to-day we may see beautiful modern examples, as for instance those upon the monument of the Altar to the Patria, where the Unknown Warrior is buried.

The whereabouts of the original golden candlesticks carried in triumph to Rome by Titus, has been the subject of much speculation. For many years a most persistent tradition located them at the bottom of the Tiber. But more accurate historical research leads us to believe that the Persians may have turned them into royal crowns,

6

jewellery for court ladies, and so forth. For, although they had been handed over by Vespasian to the virgin custodians of the Temple of Peace in Rome, afterwards, in the sack of the city, Ganseric, King of the Vandals, carried them off to Carthage with many other precious objects from Rome. Bellisario in his turn appropriated them, in A.D. 535, to embellish Byzantium (Constantinople), whence they mysteriously found their way again to Jerusalem. This time, however, they went, not to the old Temple, but to a Christian church.

In the year A.D. 614 Khosros, the barbarian King of Persia, took Jerusalem and carried off the candlesticks. Since then all trace of them has been lost. It would seem as if the curse upon the Jew had no bounds, for even the ornaments of the Temple could find no rest but wandered from land to land.

If, as we have surmised, the refined gold was partially utilised for the decoration of fair Persians of the Court, it may not be beyond the realms of possibility that on the finger of some rich, emancipated lady of that land, pointing to-day to the panels under the Arch of Titus, there may actually gleam an antique ring made from this very gold.

Before passing through the arch you may obtain your first glimpse of the Colosseum, framed, as it were, by the form of the arch. This is another of those views which cannot be forgotten, more

especially if you are fortunate enough to reach
that spot while the sun is still on the other side of
the monument. The façade towards the spectator
is then all in shadow and the Colosseum in a blaze
of light. No effort should be spared to obtain the
first glimpse of the Colosseum under these conditions. Its beauty will surpass every expectation.

With this display before us we descend the
Clivus Triumphalis and, surrounded by other ruins,
we come to an open space in front of the
Colosseum. Here stands the well-preserved Arch
of Constantine the details of which already show
signs of decadence.

The Meta Sudens or large fountain, the remains
of which are still to be seen, was for a long time
thought to be the place where the gladiators
bathed after their contests in the Colosseum. But
as a matter of fact it probably performed no more
than a purely decorative function.

Near to the Colosseum is still visible a large
base where once stood a great bronze-gilt statue.
It was a colossal figure of the comedian Nero, who
caused it to be erected before his home in the
Palatine. From its height of one hundred and
twenty feet one may perhaps imagine something of
the extravagance of his ideas.

On his well-deserved death the palace passed to
other hands, and, by order of Hadrian, the great
figure was removed to the side of the Colosseum.
It took twenty-four elephants to perform the task.

One wonders by what path all these huge beasts with their enormous burden could have made the removal. Certainly they could not have gone under the Arch of Titus, therefore we may conclude that a special road was made. I suspect that neither Carter Paterson nor Pickfords could have undertaken this enterprise!

In its progress that colossal statue must have dwarfed everything it passed, even the Colosseum must have appeared but a pillbox. Gulliver's journey to the land of Lilliput might have been suggested by the passage of this effigy of Nero through the streets of Rome.

After months of hard work the statue was re-erected, but this time the head was adorned with radiant gilt spikes to represent the sun. Later a pretentious and vain successor, Commodus, more ambitious even than Nero, decapitated the colossus and substituted his own head, quite regardless of its proportions compared with those of his " divine " predecessor.

The Church had no chance of smelting Nero into bells or candlesticks for some new and sumptuous romanesque temple. The Goths arrived before and undoubtedly turned him into coin together with the bronze they collected from those innumerable pigeon-holes we see all round the Colosseum, once containing bronze keys designed to strengthen the masonry.

CHAPTER VII

ROME : THE COLOSSEUM

No other monument in the history of art has ever been re-baptized with a more appropriate name than the Flavian Amphitheatre—now known as the Colosseum. It received this name because of the colossal figure of Nero, of which we have just spoken, and of which only the foundation remains to-day. It certainly deserves some such name if only because its enormous solidity has enabled it to survive the vicissitudes of many turbulent ages.

For economy's sake it was built by Jewish prisoners taken at the fall of Jerusalem ; and, although part of it has been demolished to erect later edifices in Rome, yet enough is left for us to judge of its original great size. It may truly be called at this day, in the words of Byron, " a noble wreck in ruined perfection ".

To give some idea of its vastness it would be sufficient to say that it was capable of containing 100,000 spectators. Rome had longed for many years for a great amphitheatre and the Emperor

Vespasian supplied the want. It was started by him in the year A.D. 72 and dedicated in A.D. 80.

It is not merely time or imagination that has exaggerated its size. Even Marcellinus, of those days, in his writings tells us " the height of the great walls of the amphitheatre so solidly built of Tiburtine could scarcely be seen by the human eye ".

The form of the edifice is elliptical, and it measures 1900 feet in circumference. Its height of 167 feet is ranged in four stories—the first Doric, the second Ionic, the third Corinthian and the fourth Composite.

As in those times the public sports were considered as indispensable to the masses almost as bread itself, the entertainments given there were devised to satisfy this sporting instinct. For nearly five centuries there was no change in this taste of Rome, so we may say that the Colosseum during this long period gave a continuous series of games of all descriptions. At first it was devoted to exhibitions of wild animals from different parts of the world, fights among themselves and fights with gladiators: to naval battles, to fighting wild beasts and finally to the martyrdom of Christians of all ages and conditions.

The naval battles are spoken of as one of the most popular sights of that time, the Roman galleys, manned by thousands of oarsmen, fighting to the death against Syracusan flotillas. Such battles terminated only when one side was annihilated and the galleys were literally floating upon a lake of human blood.

A view from the top of the Colosseum gives us a good idea of its cyclopean proportions. Standing there little imagination is required to picture those flights of steps crowded with their hundred thousand spectators frantically applauding, or, with their thumbs turned down, *pollice versu*, supporting the verdict of the Vestal Virgins. Perhaps it is for the death of a Gaulish warrior who failed in courage in his fight with a Roman opponent after having failed to catch him with his terrible net. One can almost hear again the Roman, after the final verdict of the Vestals, shouting the usual mocking excuse as he ferociously inflicted the fatal wound : " Non te peto, piscem peto " (" It is not you but the fish I want "). The reference was to the Gallic fish upon the helmet of the vanquished.

In another mood we may picture with equal ease the Venus-like form of the Christian Lidia, stretched upon a wild bull that has been caught by the horns by her faithful servant Ursus. One may almost hear the terrific roar of the lions when, the bars of their dens opened, they leap with gaping jaws upon the defenceless Christians calmly awaiting martyrdom with arms stretched towards Heaven.

How the great refinement of artistic taste displayed in every stone of that monument could ever harmonise with the equally great refinement of barbarity shown, is one of those pathological problems that will never be solved.

No pen, no word can describe the impressiveness of this place, or the tumult of emotion it inspires when visited by moonlight on a summer evening. One should go there at a late hour, when there is no fear of meeting the ordinary tourist who generally visits the monument after a good dinner and an equally good glass of wine.

The solemnity of a solitary visit in such circumstances is immense. On one of our several moonlight visits, at 1.30 A.M. on a summer's night, our enchantment was increased by the magnificent voice of a great tenor from the opera singing "Star of Eve" from Tannhauser. I can still recall those celestial notes that seemed to fall straight from Heaven—the illusion being the greater as the artiste was concealed from sight. Was he Caruso ?

Great is the Colosseum for its vastness, but much greater are the remains of the Theatre of Marcellus for their superb design, as may be seen in my painting. It is an incomparable example of the classical type of Roman architecture of the best period, and it has served as a model for the Doric, Ionic and Corinthian orders to all subsequent ages. We were simply amazed at the beautiful proportions of the three orders of columns as well as at the elegance and dignity of all the mouldings.

In the reproduction in this book it will be seen

THEATRE OF MARCELLUS, ROME

that this great relic of Roman genius is also unsurpassed for the colour it has acquired with the passing of centuries.

Not far from the Colosseum, on the slope of the Coelian Hill, where stands the picturesque Villa Coelimontana, can be seen to this day the remnants of the Fountain of Egeria. From these waters, seven centuries before the Christian era, rose the beautiful form of the Nymph Egeria when she uttered her words of fervent love and advice to her beloved King Numa, the second King of Rome.

By order of his Nymph, Numa consecrated the dark cavern from which the waters issued to the Muses. It was here, too, that the Vestal Virgins had to wash the *penetralia*, the linen of their sanctuary erected to the Goddess. Not far from that spot at the present day other linen is to be seen drying in the sun—linen much purer than that of the altar of Egeria. This is the linen of the Hospital of S. Stefano Rotondo, founded by the Blue Sisters to alleviate the sufferings of humanity.

I had heard a good deal of the self-sacrifice of these Christian Vestals who, instead of wasting time in maintaining useless burning lights, watch with inexhaustible and loving care many a living lamp that from age or sickness would without their care soon have gone out. It is to the devotion of these white and blue vestals that many a life is owed, and more especially to one—Sister Gregory—

7

a real angel in nun's clothing, whose name is as well known in England as in Rome itself.

A visit to their Hospital would remain as powerfully impressed upon the mind as one to the Colosseum. The entrance to the institution cannot be mistaken. It almost touches S. Stefano Rotondo —once a meat market, now a Christian church, and it is through one of the arches of an aqueduct that one enters, amid a veritable cascade of purple wistaria hanging from an old tree and incidentally all but obliterating a delightful gem of a marble well dating from the twelfth century. This wistaria hangs there as a banner of Nature's own providing to tell us that within are other flowers—those known as the Blue Sisters.

CHAPTER VIII

THE MARBLES OF ROME

MARCELLO, soon after he had taken Syracuse in 540 B.C., brought to Rome in great pomp a large quantity of works of art as spoils of war. This was really Rome's first opportunity of admiring works of Greek art. Marcello was perhaps the first to claim the right of despoiling the temples even of their art treasures, on the pretext of adorning those of his own gods at home. But in spite of this precedent the Romans remained for a long time much attached to the more simple tastes of their fathers. This was shown when Quinto Fulvio Flacco erected a Temple to Fortuna in acknowledgement of her protection during the war against the Celtiberi. This temple he had secretly covered with marble tiles taken from another temple—that of Junone Lacinia in the Bruzzi. This sacrilege caused great consternation in Rome, and the citizens forced the Senate to take immediate action against him. He had to appear before them and was strongly reprimanded for having done what

51

neither Piro nor Hannibal would ever have dared
to do. Orders were given for Fulvio to take back
the tiles, and sacrifices were offered to Juno in
expiation of his offence. It seems that even after
the destruction of Carthage, in the year 608, the
noble families of Rome employed only the stone
from Lazio. This is shown by a letter from Seneca,
written to Lucillo, in which he says, "I am writing
from the actual villa of Scipio the African. How
different were his habits from ours ! His house is
built of square stones from Albano—his bathroom
is small and dark as in the old times, and yet this
humble roof has sheltered the head and this
miserable floor has been trodden by the feet of the
terror of Carthage ".

As is usually the case, after a period of simplicity
came one of ostentation, not only in matters of
costume but also in things pertaining to architecture. Quinto Mitello Macedonico was the first
to adorn his villa with imported marbles and in
reproach he was surnamed " Begetter of Luxury ".

At the very beginning of this period of luxurious
decoration the building was carried out in solid
marble, and if we consider the size and number of
the remains of such buildings we must stand amazed
at the enormous amount of marble the Romans
must have extracted from their quarries. We
cease also to wonder that the quarries of the
rarest marbles soon became exhausted. Indeed, if
we go about old Rome, we see that marble is

everywhere, which of itself adequately explains why measures were taken by the Senate to restrict its use and also why high prices were paid for the privilege of working even small quarries. In fact permission to work them was sometimes withheld altogether.

The extensive use of white and coloured marbles by the Romans naturally made them experts in quarrying, cutting, polishing, and transporting it both by land and sea. Houses, forums, public baths, libraries and above all, temples were almost entirely covered either with painted decorations and mosaics, but above all with marbles.

The employment of colour, as explained elsewhere, became almost a mania with them. We can well imagine the splendid contrast provided by the white togas of the senators against the coloured marble walls of the Senate. How different from our own Houses of Parliament ! Instead of the stately magnificence of the past we are confronted with a Speaker dressed in a much less artistic style surrounded by hundreds of members in frock coats, all sombre, except where a member of socialistic leaning breaks the monotony with a red tie. And all these members form a mass of dark colour, only relieved by the shining of some bald heads and white collars and cuffs. Except for these, it is impossible to distinguish the member from the seat out of which he springs to deliver those speeches so homely after

CHAPTER IX

ROME : CHURCHES AND PALACES

IT seems as if Rome had been predestined by the will of God to be a great capital in all times. It was the capital of the old pagan world ; then the capital of Christianity, and to-day, while retaining the latter title, is also the capital of modern Italy.

If towns like Florence, Venice and Milan have a great charm of their own, Rome has a charm still greater, a charm that overshadows them all. To visit it once is to wish to do so again and again.

The classicism of old is still there, and it is wonderfully intermingled with everything and every one we meet. At each corner are seen types of men and women whom you could affirm to be reincarnations of Horatius, Caesar, Titus, Cecilia, Metella or Claudia. The spacious forehead, the large oval eye, the classically arched mouth and beautiful teeth, the profile of the nose, the column-like neck, the abundant black hair, the sonorous voice, accompanied by the declamatory move-

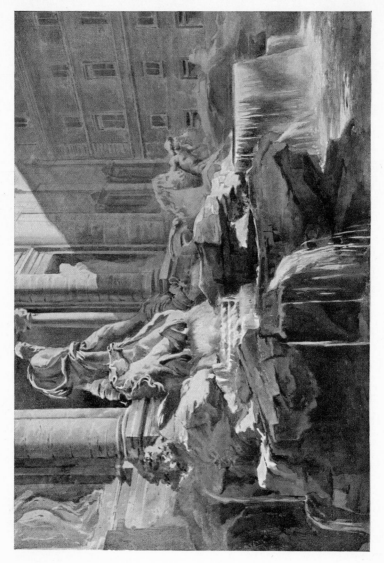

FOUNTAIN OF TREVI, ROME (page 69)

ments of the hands—all bear witness that nothing is lost of the old Latin type.

Even in the taste for amusements the classicism is noticeable, advertisements of theatrical performances like Hamlet, Aida, Rigoletto, Pagliacci are to be seen everywhere. Nor is this the case only at certain seasons, but all the year round. Seldom do you see notices of frivolous plays. The same applies to the cinema. A good tragedy ever takes precedence in Rome over even the funniest of comedies.

The spirit of classicism is still better exemplified in their gardens. The Borghese, Medici, Pamphili and Pincio gardens will give a good idea of the type most appreciated. The Romans infinitely prefer this style in spite of the fact that the *Giardino Inglese* (English Garden) has always been much appreciated. In the art and craft of garden-making indeed they easily surpass any other country.

Besides the Rome of the Kings, the Empire and the Republic, there is still another Rome, which impresses the visitor perhaps even more, the Rome of the Churches and Palaces.

Wherever you turn you are confronted with a sumptuous church or an equally fine palace. Some of these date from the best periods of art, some from the times of decadence. But all are wonderful for the tone they have acquired at the hand of Time.

At the head of about four hundred churches that

8

are to be seen in Rome, one might say at the head of all Christian churches of the world, stands, of course, St. Peter's. It is the chief glory of modern Rome. It stands on the very spot where once was the Circus of Nero, soaked with the blood of so many Christian martyrs—the " rock " upon which it is built being the head of St. Peter, which lies beneath the much-worn plate of brass under the very centre of the soaring dome.

Yes ! that is the centre where great men like Bramante, San Gallo, Fontana, Bernini and Michael Angelo above all, poured forth the best of their talents, rendering that marvel of the world eternal.

On entering the piazza you are struck with the immensity and perfect proportions of all those masses of travertino, so wonderfully shaped by genius. The colonnade and foundations by Bernini, although erected so long after the best period, represented by Michael Angelo, are nevertheless features that in themselves are grand and that harmonise well with the splendid proportions of Maderno's façade and the lines of the majestic dome behind it. Even the obelisk, which once adorned Nero's Circus, seems as if it were created for the position it holds.

But the feature that will always remain unsurpassed is the dome ; one of the greatest architectural conceptions of all ages. You can get a better idea of its beauty if you look at it from one side of the building. It is only from such a position that the dome can be seen as Michael Angelo originally conceived it. The façade was brought forward at a later date, in order to change the whole plan from a Greek to a Latin cross, and cuts with its attic the noble drum from which the dome's beautiful lines spring against the sky.

Ascending several flights of expansive steps we reach the big porch with its famous bronze portals by which the church is entered. Inside, the first impression is one of stupefaction. One feels so insignificant, an entire nonentity, the last of things in the order of God's creation. One remains rooted to the threshold. Others around are affected in the same way, unable to advance until, the first shock over, they are able to rearrange their sense of relative values.

The floor, an infinite sea of white marble, from which spring the great pillars of the nave and the four enormous piers which carry the dome, adds greatly to the grandeur of the superstructure. And when, after a long walk from the entrance, you at last come beneath the dome and raise the eyes you begin to realise why to Michael Angelo's name is added the prefix " The Divine ".

Although different ages have contributed towards beautifying the interior, yet everything is in perfect keeping with its greatness and majesty. The Baldacchino and the dome, the Chair of St. Peter supported by great bronze figures of bishops behind the High Altar, the monuments by Canova and others, the mosaics of the Evangelists under the cupola, are all things to be profoundly admired. If the northern taste of the visitor prefers Gothic to Renaissance it makes little difference, they all remain profoundly impressed.

In order to obtain a still better conception of the greatness of St. Peter's and the Vatican, we ascended the dome. The marvellous view of the Eternal City to be obtained there is almost as great as that from the Victor Emanuele monument.

Adjoining St. Peter's, the Vatican is seen as an assemblage of buildings of various styles and periods—the *tout ensemble* worthy of being considered another wonder of the world. The Sixtine Chapel by Michael Angelo, at the sight of which Raphael declared he would never paint a nude figure again ; the Stanze by Raphael himself ; the Borgia apartments by Pintoricchio ; the Pinacoteca with its Titians, Peruginos, Raphaels and Botticellis ; the Museum with its marvellous agglomeration of masterpieces, Egyptian, Etruscan, Greek and Roman ; its Library containing the rarest papyri and codices in existence, all these are comprised within that great town of learning and art called the Vatican.

While before the *torso del Belvedere*, a magnificent piece of Greek sculpture, we could almost see there Michael Angelo, feeling with his sensitive hands the beautiful form, in those last days when he could no longer see.

feet five inches in height, and all sumptuously
dressed in military uniform with cuirasses and
helmets. After a few words with a General
Aide-de-Camp to the King, I was received by
His Majesty.

He showed much interest in my art-work and
that of all other artists in England. His critical
remarks on certain productions of modern art were
most learned. I remember him talking at some
length of Alma Tadema's work, which he seemed
to know very well.

In speaking of the beauty of the Italian scenery
and of the superb monuments of art of that land,
one could see in his face the pride he had in being
King of Italy. And if he is proud of being King
of the Italians, they, on their part, are proud to
be his subjects.

Victor Emmanuel III., the King-Soldier, one of
the most accomplished men of our age, is a great ruler
and a great politician. The charming brightness
of his youth, which endeared him to all Italians,
is still there, although the cares of State, so ably
directed by his wisdom and more especially at the
time of the War, have left some traces upon his
amiable countenance.

His nobility of character, his charity, his ex-
emplary moral standard as husband and father, are
virtues that necessarily endear him to his subjects.
In fact he is the idol of all. His great judgement,
shown in the political movements of the past few

years, have been fully appreciated by all his
subjects.

Of the Queen the Italians are also justly proud.
Her work among the wounded in the war period
on the actual field of battle will never be forgotten.
Most appropriately and lovingly she has been
christened " The Consoling Angel of the Battle-
field ".

Amongst the many other churches of great
interest in Rome we should, of course, mention
that of St. John Lateran. Apart from its historic
association with the Popes it is memorable for its
poetic cloister of the tenth century, its Byzantine
apse and its mosaic floor. The latter was given
by one of the most celebrated of Roman families,
the Colonna, as a token of gratitude to God for the
great victory over the Turks at Lepanto.

The travertino façade of the church surpasses
for style and conception all others in Rome. The
adjoining museum is one of the best and most
interesting in the city.

Close to the latter is the *Scala Santa*, or Stairs of
the Palace of Pilate, much venerated by all
Christians. In the Piazza San Giovanni stands a
beautiful apse in mosaic marking the spot where
once stood the Triclinium of Constantine's palace.
At a short distance from there we visited Santa
Croce in Jerusalem, containing the principal relics
of the Christian Church.

St. Clement, built upon the house of that saint,

THE FOUNTAIN OF PIAZZA NAVONA ROME (page 69)

the second pope of Rome, is the best example of
the art of the early Christian period in Italy.
Every time we found ourselves anywhere near, in our
artistic quest, we never failed to visit it once again.

Quite close to St. Clement, built upon some
Roman remains, stands Santi Quattro Coronati,
the church of the four stone-mason martyrs. Here,
lately, beneath the whitewash upon the walls of
the chapel of the Stone-masons of to-day, they
discovered some frescoes. They are the earliest
examples of mural decoration in true fresco and
are of the greatest artistic and historic interest.

The real treasure of that church, however, is the
cloister. A charming little nun, all in white,
answered our ring. The perfect silence, only
broken by the cooing of doves and the music of a
spray of water in a fountain in the quadrangle,
impressed us so much that we could not tear ourselves away. No better place could be conceived
for a contemplative life. How pleased the little
nun looked at our involuntary enthusiasm. When
we left we told her how we envied their beautiful life ; and she replied, " Ah ! we are rich
indeed ! The treasures of gold accumulated in our
hearts beat all the banks in the world. But any-
body may become as rich as we are." The restora-
tion of this gem of architecture is the work of
Professor Munoz, to whom Rome and the archæological world owe so much.

It would be impossible here to refer to all the

9

churches we visited and it would be quite out of
the question to mention a tithe of the numerous
artistic treasures we saw therein. Mention must,
however, be made of several. There was, for
example, San Pietro in Montorio, an exquisite
specimen of architecture by Bramante, where we
saw the very spot on which St. Peter was crucified
head downwards. It is built on one of the seven
hills and commands magnificent views of Rome
and the Castelli Romani. There was San Giovanni
de Fiorentini, with its interior decoration entirely
carried out in marble—even the " pictures " being
sculptured in *alto-relievo*. There was Santa Maria
della Pace, with the beautiful Sybils by Raphael,
and San Pietro in Vincoli, with its marvellous
Moses by Michael Angelo, the latter showing the
mark where the artist, in a burst of enthusiasm,
smote the great lawgiver upon the knee saying,
" Why don't you speak " ! There was San Paolo
fuori le Mura, with its beautiful cloister, its famous
Galla Placidia mosaics, its rich interior and its
modern façade. There was Santa Maria degli
Angeli with its monolithic Roman columns, once
part of the famous baths of Diocletian ; Santa
Maria Maggiore with its two beautiful squares ;
Santa Maria in Aracocli and Santa Maria in
Trastavere with their renowned mosaics and floors.
There was Santa Maria del Popolo, a magnificent
example of fourteenth-century architecture, with
its Sansovino monuments.

BASTIONS OF SANGALLO, NETTUNO (page 70)

We concluded our visit to the churches of Rome with a moonlight pilgrimage to the Pantheon, now Santa Maria ad Martyris. The portico with its sixteen Corinthian columns, added by a Greek architect to what was once a public Roman bath, forms a majestic entrance worthy of a temple of the gods.

A full moon shining upon the metal covering of the dome and those columns casting their long shadows, rendered it still more impressive. The great bronze doors, the only remaining metal-work of ancient date, were almost closed, so that we had to enter one by one.

No more remarkable sensation can be imagined than the sight which greeted us. We were, it seemed, in a vast circular space illuminated by an enormous column of silvery light from the moon, which struck upon the floor in a great oval. The reflection from this created in the church a mysterious atmosphere of unsurpassable beauty.

And in that dim atmosphere we saw the vast dome above us resembling almost the firmament itself in vastness. Our little party being alone no distracting circumstances disturbed the profound contemplativeness into which we were plunged.

In going round those great walls, on which the dome rests, we passed in review those splendid pillars which add so much to the decorative effect. They seemed indeed like gigantic sentinels of stone guarding the dead. We saw the tombs of the two

first kings of modern Italy—Victor Emanuel and
Umberto. They are beautiful pieces of architectural design in perfect keeping with their setting
and were designed by Counts Manfredi and Sacconi.

Then in one of the chapels we paused before an
inscription which reads :

> Living, great Nature feared he might outvie
> Her works ; and dying, fears herself to die.

It was the tomb of Raphael Sanzio.

As Rome is unrivalled for her churches, so, too,
she has no equal in her palaces. Palazzo Farnese,
Palazzo della Cancelleria and Palazzo Massimo are
three architectural creations that have never been
surpassed. The palaces of the Campidoglio, by
Michael Angelo, are no mean examples of his
genius. Palazzo Venezia, with its sumptuous halls
and porches, the Palaces Doria, Borghese, Spada,
Colonna and Farnesina (with Raphael's frescoes),
are likewise most impressive in their respective
styles and beautiful by reason of the colour of their
stones.

Another characteristic of Rome is its fountains,
from which, day and night, pour forth thousands of
gallons of crystal water. A delightful episode is
told of a king invited by the Pope to the unveiling
of the two larger fountains in the Piazza of St.
Peter's. The king, whose capital was ill-supplied
with water, was concerned at the amount of water
running to waste and besought the Pope to have it

turned off now that he had seen it. Great was his amazement when he was told that the fountains were destined to play for all time.

The Fontana di Trevi is by far the most imposing, both for its architectural style and its sculpture. The illustration here will give some idea of its beauty of proportion and colouring. After St. Peter's, this fountain is *the* sight for visitors to Rome. A coin into its waters and a drink therefrom, more especially if the rite be practised by moonlight, are said to assure the visitor of another early visit to Rome.

The Fontanone di Termini and the other fountains in the Piazza Barberini, San Pietro in Montorio and the Piazza Navona or Circolo Agonale, are the next most important. That of the Circolo Agonale, represented in my painting, is by Bernini. Four seated figures at the base of the Egyptian obelisk, only two of which are to be seen in the picture, represent the four principal rivers of the world. That of the Nile, whose back is towards us, is represented as frightened at the instability and bad taste of the church in front of him, whose architect was Bernini's greatest enemy. Artists of those times were very vindictive. Indeed, Michael Angelo also indulged in revenge of a similar kind in his famous "Last Judgement", when he painted an enemy of his at the Vatican as one of the lost souls in Hell. Neither the cardinals nor the Pope could persuade the artist to remove him from those eternal torments, and to this day the guides show to the visitor that burning soul as the greatest point of interest in the fresco !

Among the pictures we most admired in Rome were those by Titian in the Borghese Gallery, more especially his "Amore Sacro e Profano", and that by Velazquez at the Galleria Doria. It would be impossible perhaps to say which of these two rendered the greatest service by his paintings to the arts of the world. They are "colossi" in the painter's craft. How superficial and commonplace are portraits by even the best artists of to-day when compared with one by Velazquez, such as his "Pope Innocenzo" at the Doria. There is form, colour, broadness of treatment, and all the other qualities that can be looked for in a painter, without sacrificing the character of the sitter. Those eyes are looking at you, that mouth is going to speak. You feel as if the Pontiff might rise from his chair and walk at any moment.

In one of our excursions from Rome we visited the old and modern Ostia, the first full of most interesting Roman remains, the second full of handsome ladies in elegant bathing costumes. Then, with a short stay at Porto d'Anzio and Nettuno, other seaside resorts of the Romans, where I painted the bastions by Sangello (full of colour, as the plate will show), we finally concluded our first visit to Rome.

During those unforgettable weeks there we

THE BALCONY OF BELLA GALIANA, VITERBO (page 73)

COURTYARD OF PALAZZO FARNESE, VITERBO (page 75)

CHAPTER X

VITERBO, TOSCANELLA, BAGNAIA

" The Town of Beautiful Fountains and Beautiful
Women ", Viterbo should also be called the Town
of Beautiful Balconies, for no other town of Italy
possesses finer ones. The balcony of Bella
Galiana, illustrated here, may give an idea of the
artistic importance of these features of old Viterbo.

They are all of the Romance Period of the tenth
or eleventh century, the time when every one, and
especially young ladies, dressed in costly brocades,
when the men folk went forth to the tournament
or to battle and fair maidens gave tokens of a
flower to inspire in them courage and hope.

Standing beneath one of these balconies one
may easily picture the proud knight, clad in shining
steel, on a spirited horse and surrounded by
a crowd of retainers, one can picture him catching
and kissing the token from the gentle hands of some
beautiful girl who leans over the parapet hung
with laurels and tapestries.

But the balcony of La Bella Galiana, besides

being a beautiful example of the architecture of that period and of the colouring powers of time, is also very interesting on account of the legend attached to it. It is said that at this balcony a girl named La Bella Galiana had daily to answer the acclamations of the Viterbesi, who were never tired of showing their admiration for her peerless beauty.

A look, a gesture, a smile from her, was all they asked, and then all went about their daily occupations.

She was the idol of Viterbo. But the cruel hand of death robbed them of their goddess while still young. The death of a king or queen could not have caused more consternation. The town was plunged for a long period into the deepest mourning and a funeral at the public expense was ordered, when the whole population turned out to render to her the last homage.

The city buried her in a tomb in the central square of Viterbo. It is not said for how many years following this the people raised their hats in passing the tomb, but what seems certain is that a mason, while repairing it, out of mere curiosity raised the lid and found it empty. The people on hearing of this sacrilege wanted to kill the man, who had to fly for his life from Viterbo.

In no other town is mediaeval architecture better represented than here. The Quartiere Pellegrino is practically as it was in the eleventh, twelfth and

PIAZZA PELLEGRINO, VITERBO

thirteenth centuries. Streets, alleys, squares and churches, ordinary houses and the palaces of the rich are all beautifully preserved. And when they are re-animated by a cinema " crowd ", dressed in period costume of the time, the illusion is complete.

Among the paintings reproduced here is one of what is probably the most important corner of one of the small squares of the town. That loggia beneath the low arch must have formed an ideal place for a quiet family meal in the heat of a summer evening.

How many Juliets we saw in imagination during the many moonlight excursions we made to those places while we stayed in Viterbo ! We saw again crowds of armed soldiers rushing under those arches to the attack or defence; the barons and parties of cavaliers doffing their cloaks to fight to the death.

While crossing an old bridge we obtained our first glimpse of the exterior of the Palazzo Farnese and through a badly-fitting door we noticed one of the most original architectural conceptions of the fourteenth century. This was the courtyard of the palace, which forms the subject of my painting. We knocked and were admitted to make its closer acquaintance.

The beautiful greenish colour of the stones, so wonderfully changed under the hands of time, has become much subdued by festoons of geraniums. It is an architectural gem, undoubtedly one of the most uncommon pieces that we saw while in Italy. It is said to have been built by an ancestor of the Alexander Farnese, Pope Paul III., who lived there with his famous sister Julia, who, for her beauty, was not second even to La Bella Galiana.

On leaving the courtyard we soon found ourselves face to face with another of the marvels of Viterbo, the Palazzo Papale, dating from the thirteenth century. For years this was the residence of the Popes and witnessed events of the greatest importance. Here were held the Conclaves in the years 1276 (when John XXI. was elected) and 1281 (when Martin was placed on the throne).

At the Conclave that elected Pope Gregory X. great trouble arose among the cardinals, who could not come to an agreement. The Captain of the People, Ruggiero Gatti, by the advice of St. Bonaventure, both very tired of the procrastination, called together the cardinals in this palace, and, without any ceremony, shut them in.

Even under these circumstances they failed to decide upon the future Pope. So they remained there, like prisoners of war, for many months. As a last resort the Captain reduced their rations, and later on even uncovered the roof. The cardinals to defeat the Captain's intention erected tents in the big hall, and even to-day large holes in the floor bear witness to the planting of tent-poles.

Finally, after thirty-three months a pope was elected—Gregory X.—and, to the gratification of the city, he gave his first benediction " in orbis et urbis " from that loggia of slender Gothic arches seen in our picture.

The experience of Gregory during those memorable days of imprisonment was such that, on his election to the chair of St. Peter, one of his first laws was concerned with the governing of conclaves.

The large red door at the top of that imposing flight of steps is the very door that Captain Ruggiero Gatti closed fast with lock and key, hence the origin of the term *con-clave*.

Of all the churches Sta. Clare of Viterbo is the most renowned. It contains the remains of the saint, and possesses a fine dome magnificently decorated by a modern artist, Giuseppe Cellini, who, in name and style, recalls the famous Benvenuto, although the one is the Cellini of painting and the other of metal-work. This dome is considered one of the sights of Viterbo.

The procession in honour of St. Clare is always a great event. An enormous pyramid, about forty feet high, thickly covered with burning candles and carried by eighty strong men, is a feature of this annual event. In many ways it recalls the procession at Velletri.

Besides the church of St. Clare there are many other churches, even more beautiful from an

architectural point of view. That of Sta. Maria
Nuova, with a delightful, octagonal external pulpit,
is perhaps the most interesting. From this pulpit
St. Thomas Aquinas preached. As there are no
steps to it a ladder had to be placed at one side to
enable the preacher to reach the pulpit.

As we have said before, Viterbo is commonly
renowned for its beautiful fountains and beautiful
women. It is an old saying, but it stands good
even to this day. For, as there is no square
without its beautiful, monumental fountain, so, we
might almost say, there is no balcony that is not
embellished at some time of the day by the beauty
of woman.

The streets, the cafés, the churches, are full of
such examples of feminine charm. La Bella
Gagliana must indeed have been a veritable goddess
of beauty to have held such undisputed sway over
the hearts of the Viterbesi.

Whilst at Viterbo we made a short stay at
Toscanella, a few miles away. We were indeed
glad we did so, for amongst the many interesting
artistic monuments, we saw two most beautiful
romanesque churches of the eleventh century.
From the interior view of one of these, that of
St. Peter, shown in our picture, some idea may be
gathered of the beauty of both. Those walls once
were literally covered with votive frescoes, now
nearly all peeled off by the rain.

For many centuries those walls stood open to the

THE CHURCH OF ST. PETER (12th Century), TOSCANELLA

weather without the covering of a roof. From the beauty of the colouring and purity of drawing exhibited by the portions still remaining, it is evident that they would have stood comparison with the finest work of their period.

The two blocks of stone-work, capped with slabs, were altars at which the priest once officiated facing the congregation. On one of the spandrels of the big arch of the nave (not shown in this picture) are represented the punishments of Hell. A large devil, calmly roasting a sinner on a spit before a ferocious fire is one of the subjects.

The exterior of the church exhibits some beautiful romanesque stone carving.

On the opposite side of Viterbo stands Bagnaia, with its unique Villa Lante. Ascending from terrace to terrace, by flights of stone steps all decorated with balustrades, statues and fountains, you reach the casino or palace. In style and colouring it is most beautiful, standing out as it does from a classic background of pines and cypresses.

From here you see below the little town all built in grey stone. One of the main roads ends with what may be termed a second Tarpean Rock, *Rupe Tarpea*, like that at the Capitol of Rome, from whence the Romans used to throw their traitors. The condemned of Bagnaia, on leaving the Palace of Justice close by, in order to escape the spears and swords of the soldiers, ran madly down the incline, and, being unable to stop at the sudden turn of the road, had to jump into the abyss below. It was this that gave the name of Via del Mal Salto—the street of the dreadful leap.

THE PAPAL PALACE, VITERBO (page 76)

CHAPTER XI

CASTELLI ROMANI

FROM the days of our youth we have been familiar
with the famous Horatii et Curiatii legend and
the strategy by which the Roman Horatius gained
the victory in the threefold duel. As we were
about to make a tour of the environs of Rome,
my friend was anxious to see the very spot where
the surviving Roman ran down the hill pursued
by the three Curiatii until, turning suddenly, he
transfixed them all.

Accordingly we decided to include Albano in our
tour round the Castelli Romani—a district about
thirty or forty miles from the city, which, to the
modern Roman, as well as to many a foreigner, is
not less famous for its exquisite wines than for its
historic legend.

We planned this excursion very carefully and
decided to go as far as possible by tram-car. It was
a glorious day when we started, if possible better
than any we had experienced previously. In ten
minutes we had reached San Giovanni Laterano,

where we passed through the old Roman gate of that name. As by magic we found ourselves face to face with a scene that could only be compared to an earthly paradise. It was the celebrated Campagna Romana, the beauty of which surpasses every expectation. Solemn stillness reigned throughout that immensity, broken only by the melodious singing of the birds. Field after field gave subtle gradations of green toned and still further diversified with patches of wild flowers in infinite variety. Uninterrupted by hedges, so familiar a feature of the English countryside, these fields stretched out before our eyes like an interminable luxurious carpet, as a background there were the Tusculan and Alban hills. No artist could ever conceive anything so beautiful in form and so exquisitely toned in blues.

Here and there the scene was dotted with charming villages, some perched up in seemingly inaccessible places, others on the slopes which incline gently to the plain. To the right is Porto d'Anzio on the shores of the Mediterranean, to the left is the imposing range of the Apennines, with Tivoli, Villa d'Este, and Hadrian's Villa half concealed among the fragrant woods of old oaks and chestnuts.

Running parallel to the old Via Appia, with its marvellous remains, monuments erected to the memory of the great among men, we get well into the heart of the Campagna. We are accompanied all the way by the broken line of the superb arches of the Aqueducts. Even to-day the waters of Rome are celebrated for their purity and freshness, just as they were in the days of Claudius, when these monumental water-ducts were in full use.

It was by means of sixteen lines of such arches that Rome was supplied with its pure waters and the rich land of the Campagna irrigated. Pliny tells us that " if we consider with accuracy the quantity of water supplied to the public baths, fountains, fish ponds, artificial lakes, galley-fights (in the Colosseum), pleasure-gardens, and to nearly every home in Rome, and then think of the many obstacles that had to be surmounted, besides the distance from which the waters had to be brought, undoubtedly we must admit that nothing so great as those aqueducts can be seen in the whole world ".

The seemingly interminable line of arches springs up at intervals from the intense green of the fields, throwing transparent blue shadows on the sward. The ruins, sometimes from twenty to thirty feet high, and at others almost crumbled to the ground level, form the predominant characteristic of the Campagna.

It is through these arches that the seeker after beauty may enjoy delightful peeps at the Sabine, Tusculan and Alban hills, framed in the arches themselves. Thus in our journey we are offered thousands of exquisitely arranged pictures, with Nature herself as the artist.

We leave on the right the Acqua Santa with its golf-links and racecourse and later on the aerodrome —all so terribly incongruous in proximity to the classicism of the surroundings. Here the new Appian Way joins the old Via Appia, and we proceed in an almost straight line, always ascending, towards Albano.

Then we pass innumerable vineyards loaded with bunches of exquisite red and golden grapes. At intervals we encounter still further remains of Rome's greatness in the past, springing up as if by magic amidst the products of the bountiful earth.

Only a few hundred yards from the Albano gate is supposed to be the spot where the chief war between the Horatii and Curiatii took place. Here we stopped and, giving our imagination free play, we reconstructed a mental picture of the historic encounter.

Out of the two hostile opposing armies six of the most powerful men were selected, three from each, to determine the destiny of their adjoining countries. At a given signal these men approached each other and then ensued a " war " which, contrary to what we are accustomed to expect, ended the inter-racial dispute in a few minutes. The victory of the Romans, consummated without any long armistice or parley of any sort, is unique perhaps in the annals of war. The two armies fraternised and together descended to Rome as one, increasing still more the prestige of the city.

After all, had the Romans lost the day and become the vassals of the Curiatii, they would yet have absorbed the less virile race. The name of Rome was already too great and fascinating to be either forgotten or suppressed. What a contrast with the present-day method of warfare ! How much wiser were the Horatii and Curiatii !

As we stood there pondering the astute strategy of the Romans we turned our heads, and there we saw from the great height a reversed panorama from the one we saw from the San Giovanni Gate on leaving Rome. The same extensive green fields, one after the other, the Aqueducts, the Via Appia, the Cecilia Metella seemed almost, as it were, under our feet, and all dissolved in transparent blue mist.

Little by little everything in the distance became involved in the blue mantle, until finally, almost on the horizon, like a beam of incandescent light, stretched the marvellous outline of the Eternal City, the civiliser of the world. The imposing dome of St. Peter's was beautifully outlined against the still softer blue of the Sabine hills, as if solemnly watching over the destinies of the world.

It seemed as if everything around, from the tiniest blade of green to the profound blue of the sky, spoke to us of the great men who once trod that historic Appian Way, and who at the sight of Rome must have felt their hearts beat faster with emotion.

No matter how great your country, no matter how proud you may be of your attainments or those of your ancestors, when you are confronted with so imposing and historic a view you must feel that you are, after all, but an insignificant member of that vast crowd, humanity. And yet, while you may feel humiliated before so wonderful a display of beauty and greatness, as a consolation you remember that man is the only link between matter and God.

We are now at Albano, a town full of Roman remains, with great palaces and gardens of the sixteenth and seventeenth centuries. It has been one of the favourite summer resorts of every age. Ascending, by a beautiful avenue of centenarian oaks through which there are further exquisite glimpses of Rome and the Campagna, we reach Castel Gandolfo, once the *villeggiatura* or summer residence of the Popes. Il Palazzo del Papa adjoins the little village and, on one hand, looks towards Rome, while on the other it looks towards the large lake which bears the name of Albano. From the fine gardens, always through thick chestnuts and oak-woods, you descend to the lake, which like that of Nemi was once the crater of an extinct volcano.

Up to the year 1870 the palace was regularly used by the Popes, but after the summer sojourn of Pius IX. in that year no other Pope made use of it. It has been occupied at intervals by cardinals

Romani is sent into Rome by cart and not by rail. It is found to be cheaper. It is a very picturesque sight to see the procession of wine-carts descending the hills or crossing the Campagna.

Each cart consists of a flat body upon two wheels as tall as a man. A species of small collapsible hood of goat-skin is fixed in front under which the driver sits, or sleeps practically all the way to Rome, where they arrive about daybreak. The horses have, at the point of one of the shafts, a big bundle of hay on which they feed during their long and monotonous journey. Quantities of small bells hang from the hoods and necks of the horses causing a noise that can be heard from a great distance. All the woodwork of the vehicle is painted with minute designs in bright colours, and the inside of the hood is decorated with religious pictures as a protection against robbery and the other evils of the journey. A little Pomeranian dog, always on the look-out, sits on top of the cargo as an incorruptible guardian, and it would be impossible to approach the cart without this little sentry giving the alarm.

In the silence of the night you hear the bells and the dogs for miles ; the sounds increase as they approach, rising to a deafening clamour as the cavalcade passes, and falling again as it goes into the distance. These wine-carts and the aqueducts are undoubtedly the two most characteristic notes of the Campagna.

Grottaferrata, like Farfa in Sabina or Subiaco and Monte Cassino, was a great centre of learning in mediaeval times. It now consists only of a few houses and a great girdle of colossal bastions erected for the defence of the Greek church of St. Nilo with its enormous monastery.

At the time of the great persecution by the Iconoclasts, when led by the Eastern Emperor Leo IV., a great many religious foundations fought with great vigour the orders of that emperor. But eventually they had to leave the East, and many settled permanently in the adjoining countries of the Adriatic coast, principally on the Italian side. Consequently many of them penetrated right into the peninsula, reaching almost the gates of Rome. It was a group of these religious men, with St. Nimus at their head, that settled at Grottaferrata about the tenth century. Soon after their arrival they erected the Badia or Abbey at this place, with the monastery which grew later to be, as we have said before, one of the principal seats of learning in Central Italy.

The ancient artistic traditions brought over by those learned Fathers have never been lost at St. Nimus, where even to-day there is a school of illumination and where, as at Monte Cassino, the art of illuminating still flourishes. Rare old manuscripts are still preserved in the library of the monastery.

On arrival one crosses the bridge over a moat

and enters a courtyard by a great door in a massively fortified curtain wall, beyond which is a large cloister whose colonnade supports a building of great architectural beauty. Mounting to the first floor one finds oneself in a long corridor (a characteristic monastic feature) with, on either side, many little cells occupied by the monks. Here when we made our visit the monks, both young and old, were all occupied in painting and illuminating with infinite care big missals and other manuscripts on vellum.

We entered one of these cells and had a most interesting conversation with a young monk whose work we much admired for its exquisite drawing and colouring. The mysticism upon the faces in the halo of cherubs upon which at the time he was employed, and on the face of the artist himself, struck us most forcibly. In fact we wondered if perhaps he had painted them while kneeling, as Beato Angelico painted the glory of angels in the Chapel of the Spagnoli in Florence. If it had not been for his habit one might have supposed him another St. Francis of Assisi.

We also visited the library, very rich in manuscripts of early periods, some with fine initials wonderfully illuminated in rich gold, and others with splendidly painted miniatures. The lettering was in no way inferior in artistic beauty to the pictures.

On the way downstairs we were introduced to

the Father Superior, a man of about sixty, full, equally, of humility and authority. He instructed our ecclesiastic guide to be sure to show us everything of interest, which he did, until, with a most obsequious bow, which we returned not quite so deeply, he left us and we proceeded to the Abbey.

St. Nilo was built in the seventh century, principally with the remains of old Roman temples, and it has all the characteristics of the usual Byzantine church of that period—a nave and two aisles and an apsidal termination with semi-dome covered with mosaics.

During the course of centuries, and more especially in the sixteenth and seventeenth, all the walls, even then partially stripped of their marbles, were completely denuded and plastered all over. The rich golden ceiling was erected to cover the primitive one of wood. So that to-day only the mosaics of the apse, the row of columns and the pavement are all that is left of the primitive interior decoration.

Being of an Orthodox community the church has a screen of marble, in which are two doors, dividing the sanctuary from the nave, and the High Altar stands at the back of the screen. The most notable features of the interior are the mosaics of the apse and some frescoes by Domenichino. Outside the principal feature is the ninth-century campanile, all in brick of mellow terra-cotta tone. The façade also is in brick, and has a great central doorway adorned with magnificently carved marble facings taken from some Roman temple of the best period.

Near the monastery once stood Cicero's Villa full of beautiful works of art and a rich library. All the great intellects of his time visited him there and debated with him on highest philosophical subjects. And it was those discussions that inspired him to write one of his great works, *Tusculum Disputationis*, entitled from the territory on which his Villa stood. The subjects treated comprise Contempt of Death ; Bearing Pain ; Grief of Mind ; Other Perturbations of the Mind ; and Whether Virtue be Sufficient for a Happy Life. He was scarcely given time to revise his volumes, for soon after came from Rome the barbarous news of his most unjust banishment.

After having spent some delightful hours admiring the artistic treasures of Grottaferrata, we mounted our donkeys and proceeded upon our way to Frascati.

What a contrast between the two towns ! One is a town of learning, of high intellectual refinement—a town built for God ; the other a town of pleasure, built for the worship of mammon. The old *Tusculum*, founded long before Rome was built, as also the many magnificent villas of the sixteenth and seventeenth centuries, was only erected for the pleasure-seeking population of Rome. The present town is situated on the declivity of the hill, near to the old Tusculum, and affords us another charming view of the Alma Città and Campagna Romana. The fact that it is only eleven miles from Rome makes it easy of access. A modern Roman, in fact, will say to his friend, especially perhaps on a summer evening, " Let us go to Frascati to have a glass ". As a matter of fact, in little more than a couple of hours you may get there and back in a comfortable train or tram-car.

Frascati is dotted all over with some of the most beautiful and romantic villas of Italy. The Villa Aldobrandini, of the ancient Borghese family, is the most important. Of great beauty also are the Villa Mondragone, Villa Taverna, Villa Ruffinella and Villa Torlonia. Being all laid out upon the slope of the hill they exhibit the skilfulness of their architects in making the most of such unrivalled opportunities for scenic display. Each has a sumptuous palace with its terraces and steps and fountains decorated with sea-horses, tritons playing with smiling naiads, all half-concealed under the contorted and mossy branches of ancient oaks, pines and dark cypresses.

After long rambling under those shady trees suddenly you come upon openings leading to wide terraces embellished with beautifully weather-beaten balustrades, marble statues, and seats where you may rest and admire the marvellous panorama.

There is such an old-world atmosphere about the place that one needs little help from the imagination to repeople it with visions of the past. A picture rises from the mists of time. Ladies with powdered hair and painted faces, richly clad in garments of silk and brocade that scarcely cover the gentle contour of their shoulders, are seen walking arm in arm with cavaliers in equally costly dress and bright-coloured breeches.

Hardly an inch of the dress of either sex is free from an abundance of rich laces dropping in graceful folds. Diamonds, pearls and gold shine from the heads and white bosoms of the ladies, from their fingers, and from the handles of the swords and shoe-buckles of their admirers. It is a *fête galante* that would have charmed a Watteau. We note the extravagantly courteous expression of the gentlemen, accompanied as it is by the still more extravagantly low bending of their bodies as they pay their compliments to the fair ones. The gentle pressure of the right hand upon the hilt of their swords, as they bow, raises aloft the point of the scabbard, beautifully decorated with precious stones, so that it may be seen and admired.

The appearance of a scarlet spot that is moving among the trees in the distance suddenly puts an end to this scene of gallantry. It is the Cardinal and his court, invited by the distinguished host and hostess, their excellencies the Prince and Princess Aldobrandini. Every one becomes serious and composed. Some of the cavaliers in a great flurry brush from their velvet coats some of the suspicious

13

marks of white powder left by the too great proximity of the red and white cheeks of a Contessina.

His Eminence passes by, giving a suspicious but most benevolent smile to the Conti and Contessine, Duchi and Duchessine. Soon after his scarlet robes disappear among the trees the frivolities begin once more.

A bell is heard announcing the arrival of the guest of honour. Quantities of serving-men in scarlet make room on the great terrace to let His Eminence pass. The Prince, Princess and Principessina all approach in great haste to greet him. They all bend the knee and kiss his ring. He is conducted to the place of honour, and there he sits between the host and hostess.

Soon after his arrival a long procession of attendants starts from a great marquee close by, carrying all sorts of refreshments. The glitter of the sunlight upon the magnificent service of gold as it is moved is simply dazzling. It kills even the sparkle of the ladies' diamonds.

A silvery voice, accompanied by a spinette and a 'cello, is heard close by and all turn in that direction. It is that of the young Princess in whose honour the reception is given. While she is yet singing the wonderful water-effects are turned full on. Jets spring skywards from the most unexpected places, while from the very top of a wide avenue descending from a hill a great cascade starts pouring torrents of water, which passing from basin to basin finally reaches the lake. All are amazed at their splendour—even the Cardinal congratulates the Prince.

The dream of the past melts away, but we remain there still in contemplative mood. The soft voices of those cascades, as clear as crystal, the melodious and incessant singing of the birds, the dark and mysterious shadows of the oaks and the laurels, the quivering of the patches of sunlight on the dead leaves on the pathway, all contribute to make us feel we would like to stay there and dream for ever.

But it is getting late. The donkeys and the guide are down in the square waiting for us. We must say good-bye to this charming spot, else darkness will overtake us on our way to Nemi.

CHAPTER XII

NEMI AND VELLETRI

HAD it not been for the great experience of our guide, who took us by some *real* short cuts, by the edges of precipices and through thick woods, we should have arrived at our destination late in the night. But, as it was, we emerged from the shadows of the last wood just at sunset.

What a change of scenery! What surprises, one following the other! We were not yet at Nemi when we had the first glimpse of the lake with its high ridges adorned by those classically outlined pine forests through which we see on the left the majestic castle and on the right the old Genzano.

In a few hours, we may say, we have passed backward through the centuries—from seventeenth-century Frascati to Nemi of the golden age of Rome—from decadence to the best period of Rome's artistic taste. It was on these celebrated waters of Lake of Nemi, a thousand and twenty-two feet above the sea-level, that the Roman Emperors held sumptuous festivities in honour of their goddess Diana.

Even to-day you may see the remains of that temple, erected in the old crater almost on a level with the waters. Its ruins spring up in the midst of orchards, orange groves and strawberry beds of remarkable productivity. The strawberries especially are of a flavour surpassing those from any other spot. The exquisite aroma they give forth is so strong that it is noticeable at a considerable distance. Regular consignments of them are sent to Rome every evening during the season. They are small, luscious, and as red as corals.

Much has been written by Latin poets of the beauty of Lake of Nemi; they give us graphic descriptions of Diana's festivals. The original name, *Lacus Nemorensis*, was superseded by the much more poetic *Speculum Dianae* or Diana's Mirror. But to-day it is generally known as the Lago di Nemi: a letter addressed to " Speculum Dianæ " would never reach there except by some special inspiration on the part of the General Post Office of Rome.

Great feasts were given on the lake by the Emperors. The calm waters used to touch the very steps of the temple, and vestals and priests, all in white garments, were carried in fine galleys on the waters. While all faces were turned to the temple, incense and precious spices were burned on portable altars in honour of the beautiful and youthful goddess Diana.

We can picture that procession of barges all decorated with gilded bronze, like those in the museum of the Terme Diocleziane. Full of beautiful vestals, singing and burning roses and incense to the goddess, the Chief Priest sacrifices a lamb on the altar. From the latter a thin wisp of white smoke gently rises into the perfect stillness of a summer sky, while the sound waves produced by silvery voices of the virgins echo and re-echo in the marvellous acoustic properties of that crater.

In contrast to the purity of that scene are the barges with the Emperor and his court who follow, banqueting and revelling in the most licentious manner—likewise in honour of the Bella Diana.

The morning after our arrival we visited the castle which after many vicissitudes has now become the property of Princess Ruspoli—a charming American lady full of good taste and admiration for art and nature's beauty. In company with her equally charming niece she spends there the greater part of the year.

Like a colossal eagle, shielding its young from danger, the castle crouches over the tiny houses beneath it, to protect them from the attack of an enemy. Its many towers and embrasures speak eloquently of the fact that, in the old days, the castle must have been a very necessary adjunct to safety.

Another most advantageous position, whence

procession is transformed into an enormous bazaar. Every shop sells votive candles of all sizes, from the thinnest and shortest that cost as little as sixpence, to those six or seven feet long, highly decorated with gilt patterns and sacred pictures, costing as much as £3 a piece. You see these candles displayed for sale in every shop, standing amongst the most incongruous articles imaginable. You see them amongst sacks of flour, loaves of bread, cooking utensils, lines of thickly-soled boots, women's skirts and lingerie, men's coats and trousers, harness for horses, cheeses and long decorative festoons of sausages. And around this enormous display of wax in the shops you see groups of women, just arrived from the surrounding villages, all eagerly contemplating or bartering for the possession of candles.

A girl of eighteen with most beautiful features and large eyes was in one of these groups. She was nearly crying as she argued with an old Jew over the price of a particularly fine candle—even the Jews on this occasion sell candles for the Madonna ! I gave him an expressive look, meaning that I would pay the difference, and he let her have the candle at the supposed reduced price. Having slipped into his ready palm the difference between the price he had asked and that she had been able to pay, I ventured to speak to the girl. I was curious to know why she bought so expensive a candle. In a most pathetic voice she made answer,

" Big is the candle and big is the sacrifice I make
to obtain a miracle through the intercession of the
Madonna ". I ventured further to ask her what
grace she was beseeching. " That *he* may return
to me ", was her simple reply. She wiped the tears
from her cheeks and soon disappeared in the crowd.

I followed with the eye the top of that candle
moving along through the crowd with great speed
until eventually it was lost to view.

If only those big candles could speak how
much more tender our hearts would grow! What
pitiful stories they would tell us of the fast-beating
hearts against which they are so closely clasped
during the procession, of the promises they have
heard, of the pale faces upon which they have cast
their yellow light.

Scores of them burn for the return to the faith
of some son who has gone astray! Scores for
keeping hearts faithful to those for whom they
have sworn everlasting love !

Suddenly beautiful music is heard in the distance.
Every one turns—" Che cosa è, che cosa è ? " (what
is it?) they ask one another. It is the band of the
grenadiers who march at the head of the procession.
Guns are fired. The bells of every church ring
out with redoubled energy, especially those of
S. Clemente which actually commenced to ring at
four o'clock in the morning. How the ringers
could continue ringing for so many hours amazed
us. But a short visit to the ground floor under the

tower of S. Clemente after the function was over
revealed the secret. This lower room of the belfry
is literally transformed into a big bed with a straw
mattress. On this several ringers recline flat on
their backs and pull the ropes. The latter, in
their turn, with the tremendous power acquired
by the swing of the great bells, pull the *campanari*,
or bell-ringers, up off their bed and nearly off their
feet. Then with another swing down again on to
their backs on the bed go the ringers. As this
species of gymnastics cannot be endured for very
long, the ringers are changed every hour.

The sun was just setting, and as we wished to
see the procession under the most favourable
conditions, namely as it returned to the Cathedral,
we waited at the Corso Vittorio Emanuele near S.
Martino.

During the day the clouds began to assemble
over the hills and every one began to be somewhat
doubtful of the success of the procession, more
especially when the rumblings of thunder were
heard in the direction of Monte Circeo, which
invariably indicates bad weather, if not a terrific
storm.

We took a window at the spot we had selected,
from which we could obtain a commanding view
of the procession as it approached down the Corso.
The houses were a mass of festooned flags and
Venetian lights, known as *lanternoni*. Each house-
holder, in honour of the occasion, does his best to

surpass his neighbour in display if not in good taste.

After the military band comes a large crucifix, twenty feet high, kept steady by stalwart men all dressed in white and blue, each showing great pride in his performance. Next, a group of little girls, dressed like angels ; then boy-scouts in uniform, headed by their buglers. At a short interval follows another group of angels—this time somewhat more grown-up, with flaming rosy wings and laurel wreaths ; then the servants of the municipality (if the party in power at the time is not socialistic). Several groups of girls from various colleges follow, all dressed in their distinctive costumes. With another band here starts the stream of women, all in black and with bare feet.

These women, indeed, form the most touching portion of the long procession. They have come from far-away places with great candles in their arms or across the shoulders. Others one may see with a candle in one arm and a suckling baby in the other, with which burdens they may have descended from far among the rocky mountains. The greater number of these women indeed have come thus from many miles away, covering in their unshod feet the distance that separated them from their venerated Madonna delle Grazie.

To see all those naked white feet beneath black skirts as they move to the solemn rhythm of the

music is a most touching sight, one that would move
the hearts of the many otherwise indifferent
spectators almost to tears. All these, each without
exception carrying a candle, drop grease every
step of the way, more especially on their neighbours.

After the women there follow more banners,
more candles, and then, at the end of what may
be likened to a great fiery serpent winding down
the hill, appears the *Macchina*, surrounded by the
clergy in their rich copes of gold and silver tissue.
It is carried on two very long poles by some forty
men, and consists of a portable altar surmounted
by a large ornamental silver frame containing the
picture of Mary with the Holy Child painted by
St. Luke, all adorned with costly jewels. Long
strings of pearls, rubies and diamonds practically
cover up all the picture except the faces and hands
of the figures. Gendarmes in parade uniform
closely surround the *Macchina* and clergy for their
protection. Another military band, followed by
thousands of people, closes the procession.

It was still passing under our window when the
storm which had been threatening all the afternoon broke with most terrific violence. The steep
Corso Vittorio Emanuele was transformed in a
few moments into a formidable torrent. The little
white angels with their crowns of flowers; the
women with their bare feet, their candles and their
babies; the bands with their big drums and shining
brasses; the clergy in their costly robes, all took

hasty refuge in the nearest shops, even in a café, a tobacconist's, or a public-house.

In great haste the *Macchina* with the Madonna and some of the clergy took shelter under the porch of a church. The tall standards and enormous crucifix were placed in divers corners of the street. To add to the confusion the electric lights, both in the streets and in the houses, went out, and the town was left in complete darkness — only a few of the Venetian lights of coloured tissue paper remained burning. Every one, half terrified, waited patiently for the light to come back.

It did so eventually, but not until half an hour had passed ; and when it did one could see, in every corner, heaps of religious implements, candle-sticks, images, crosses, all leaning against the walls awaiting the cessation of the storm.

The big crucifix, for the honour of carrying which the men had perhaps actually fought, was left all alone in a corner under a deluge of rain to remind us that, after all, the present generation is little if any better than Christ's friends and disciples were on that terrible night when He Himself was abandoned and denied even by His best and most courageous apostle, Peter.

After the storm came calm. The thunder ceased. Each, after putting out a hand to find if it had ceased to rain, once more takes position in the slowly reforming procession. The candles are re-kindled, the priests start anew to sing with great

CARYATIDES IN VILLA GINNETTI, VELLETRI (page 105)

animation, the people respond with great fervour, the bands play louder than before and the whole fiery snake-like procession begins again to move slowly forward.

Amongst the thousands of people forming that procession I recognised the beautiful girl whom we had met a few hours earlier purchasing a candle. In that yellow candle-light by which, according to an old Italian proverb, " neither woman nor linen should ever be bought " (*nè donna nè tela da comprarsi a luce di candela*), the girl looked if anything more beautiful than ever. She was still holding her big candle, but in quite a different way from everybody else.

Her head, her features might well have been compared with those of a Venus. Some irresistible impulse of fascination made me rush down to the street and I followed her to the church door. She still sang " Madonna mia, pray for me " ! but in her every word was the prayer " Bring him back to me " ! Had I known where " he " was at that moment I could willingly have gone to the end of the world to bring him back to her.

After a noisy dinner at a restaurant, where we enjoyed more of the celebrated Velletri wines, we retired to rest, to be ready to start again next morning.

Almost at the last minute we decided again to change our mode of progress. The road in front of us was much better, so we left behind the humble donkeys, who gladly returned to Albano and we continued from here by motor. Our programme was to see Cori and Ninfa in the same day and to sleep at Terracina, whence we intended to return to Rome.

GREEK TEMPLE OF HERCULES, CORI (page 116)

CHAPTER XIII

CORI, NINFA, TERRACINA

WE reached Cori Basso in less than an hour, after having stopped at the half-abandoned Giulianello for only a few minutes. In another quarter of an hour we were in the square of Cori Alto. Cori, as a matter of fact, lies on the side of a very high hill, and is divided into Lower and Upper Cori.

Although the whole population call themselves Coresi, yet there is a great rivalry between the two ; so great indeed that they often come to blows. The result of such contests is awaited with as much interest as a cockney awaits the result of a boxing bout. The chief difference perhaps is that at Cori the " players " do not use boxing gloves, and consequently the finish is very often painful for some of the competitors.

It is at Cori Alto that one meets with the most important remains of Greek and Roman civilisation. Here is one of the best examples in Italy of cyclopean walls. From the position of these, right at the summit of the mountain, we naturally come to the

115

conclusion that at one time Cori must have been
the stronghold of some very powerful race, probably
Greek. Of course the Romans, with their usual
pride of race, did not like to admit that there had
ever been in the world any race more powerful
than they. So they upheld the fable that these
walls had been built by giants of supernatural
origin and power, beings having only one eye in
the forehead (as described by the Greeks), and
known as Cyclops.

As a matter of fact the men who built the walls
were a race much more advanced in mechanical
knowledge than the Romans,—a knowledge that
enabled them to raise up these titanic stones to
such an altitude.

The most important of all artistic remains in
Cori is, however, the Greek temple of Hercules, most
beautiful in its proportions and remarkably well
preserved. From the reproduction you may gather
something of the uncommon beauty of its colonnade.
If it were not for some freshly broken pieces which
reveal the natural colour of the stone, one might
well imagine it to be a building of lead. Its extraordinary tone is the more noticeable in contrast
with the stones now exposed below by the removal
of the broad flight of steps originally leading up to
the portico. The large and dark shadows cast by
the foremost columns and entablature, broken by
the rear columns, gives us a most telling picture,
unique of its kind. They help to emphasise the full

elegance of the demi-fluted columns with their refined Doric capitals.

Large patches of geraniums grow on some steps below, and with their bunches of flaming flowers and green leaves, serve to make the tone of the columns still more lead-like, producing a beautiful contrast with the deep blue of the sky beyond.

In the church built on the very foundation of the temple a fine example of a Roman sacrificial altar is preserved. It is a fine piece of carving, and may be considered one of the finest examples dating from the Golden Age of Rome.

The town is full of Roman remains which crop up most unexpectedly everywhere. We see odd columns supporting the corners of houses, beautifully carved cornices adorning the doors of humble cottages, or utilised as front door-steps.

Besides Greek and Roman remains there are many beautiful Gothic houses like the one illustrated here. From a picture like this it will better be realised how truly beautiful is the colouring imparted to those stones by the " great master " Time. In them one may find exquisite blendings of all the colours of the palette.

After two whole days spent in painting, with beautiful weather all the time, we removed our tents and descended the steep hill *en route* for Terracina. Magnificent views were ever spreading out before our eyes.

We broke our journey for several hours at Ninfa,

where I stayed to paint the mediæval castle so
striking in its colouring as well as by reason of the
reflection of its crumbling walls in the calm waters
that surround it.

The remains of Ninfa are all half submerged in a
marsh and are chiefly interesting to the artist for
their picturesque ruined condition and the beautiful
effects obtained by their being mirrored in the
stagnant waters around. A rich tangle of vegeta-
tion seems ever striving to make more beautiful
these relics of man's past activities, hiding the ravages
of time and making every stone picturesque. The
whole scene inspires one with thoughts of sadness,
helping one to realise how even towns, like men,
are doomed to pass away.

Finding it difficult to secure anywhere a place
to spend the night we took the last train to Terracina
and on our way passed close under Sermoneta,
which rests on the ridge of a tremendously high
rock forming a perpendicular cliff not unlike
Gibraltar.

Sermoneta was the birthplace of one of the oldest
families in Italy—that of the Dukes of Caetani of
Sermoneta. Not the least among the scions of this
noble house was the venerable Duke Sermoneta
whose death occurred only a few years ago.

Had we not been warned previously of the
difficulty of getting up to Sermoneta we should most
willingly have spent a night on this height. But
we longed for a good bed and consequently

RUINS OF MEDIAEVAL CASTLE AT NINFA

decided to go straight on to Terracina, where the bracing sea air and the proximity of Monte Circeo help to instil into one new life.

At Terracina we are in a thriving watering-place that can be seen at a glance. The fashionable ladies, the big cafés, with their tables all spread outside, the military band in the main square, all contribute to the impression. Trains full of people arrive morning and evening, returning to Rome almost empty. The fresh arrivals have to find rooms, but if one has not made some previous arrangements one may be sure of having to sleep on the sands. In fact many improvident people on the hot summer nights in the season have to accommodate themselves under porches or in the dark foundation arches of what may have been one of the many palaces of Nero.

As we know this Emperor had palaces everywhere, some of which had to be erected at ridiculously short notice, unless the contractors with whom the work was placed were willing to run the risk of being selected for testing some new method of torture.

No great imagination is required to picture the fuss and bustle—and horror—that would arise from Nero's sudden decision to spend a day (with his beautiful Poppoea) at some seaside place such as Porto d'Anzio, Nettuno or Terracina.

Chariots of all sizes at a mad speed doubtless preceded the Imperial party with every description of paraphernalia for preparing a sumptuous repast on the spot. His imperial appetite was never content with such plebeian dishes as cold leg of mutton or chicken. In fact cold meat was, in his estimation, only fit for the lions and tigers in the Colosseum. They indeed had plenty, especially at the times of the persecution of the Christians. Litters must have been used to carry the clumsy body of the divine Caesar from the nearest accessible point for his chariot up to the spot under the pines where, to this day, we see the ruins of a great palace.

And there, after an elaborate meal, half intoxicated, we may picture him calling, with a patronising gesture, his faithful tyrant Tigellinus and telling him, " See that by next August a worthy palace is built on this very spot, where I can finish my verses on the Destruction of Troy, and thus refine our poetry so abominably debased by Virgil and his school ! "

Thereupon another palace, perhaps more grand than any hitherto, was built on the spot, at public expense, and by the next August Nero's court was actually removed to the new seaside resort, and his courtiers, including his favourite, Poppoea, had perforce to find recreation in patiently listening to Nero's rasping voice and horrible versifying.

Almost touching the mainland and facing Terracina rises Monte Circeo and its classic pine woods, once the abode of the beautiful enchantress Circe,

MEDIAEVAL PORCH, VIA LAURIENTI, CORI

who, with her songs, allured mariners, young and
old, who by ill-luck struck those rocks. Her power
of attraction, Mark Twain, had he lived at that time,
would undoubtedly have estimated at thousands of
horse-power. Homer speaks of her in his immortal
Odyssey ; how Ulysses escaped being turned into
a pig, like his companions, by a wonderful drug
given him by Hermes, and how he threatened to
kill Circe, so that she changed them into men
again, younger and handsomer than before.

In spite of her dangerous reputation, Ulysses
spent a whole year in amorous union with Circe, by
whom he had a son called Telegonus. Ulysses,
arguing presumably that people of high stations
have always been excused even worse conduct than
his, made up his mind to leave Circe. So one
morning, packing up his bundle of clothes (very
scanty in those classic times, especially in the case
of gods), and with Circe's consent he started on his
way back to Greece. Arriving there, after a call
at the Lower Regions and his terrible experience
between Scylla and Charybdis, he found his beloved
Penelope had squandered all his money.

Circe, probably very glad to be rid of him,
carried on her trade of wrecking and despoiling
sailors and of turning people into all manner of
quaint beasts. Circe and Ulysses have passed
away, but one of the former's most renowned abodes,
that of Monte Circeo, is still to be seen, with its
familiar contour, its olive and orange groves and

its reflection in the waters to inspire for ever dreams of beauty like those of the immortal Homer.

The old Terracina is upon a hill and notable Roman remains are to be seen there, mingled with those of mediaeval times. In my painting is shown a typical piece, with the classical columns of a temple surmounted by what must have been, in the Middle Ages, a tower of defence like those so often seen in other towns of Italy.

As Terracina was so far from Rome (the nearest place from which in ancient times assistance could be obtained), the landowners had to fortify their own positions. Nor was it solely against neighbours, equally powerful and always to be dreaded, that they had to protect themselves ; but even more often they were called upon to resist the regular robbers who at that time were very numerous indeed.

From another illustration you may form an idea of the character and picturesqueness of Old Terracina. The beautiful Roman column and broken plinth, the noble arch which stands in defiance of the destroying hand of Time, so exquisitely coloured by the passing of many centuries, seems as if they had been expressly set there by the hand of a master scenic artist. This arch, with its graded tones of warm colour, forms as it were a frame in which we see a picture of another period, that of Romanticism,—small stairs and windows, the stilted arch which again in its turn frames

ROMAN AND MEDIAEVAL RUINS, TERRACINA (page 122)

the brilliant blue of the sky and the sea in the distance.

The frescoed Madonna, of the seventeenth century, just seen between the two arches, so different in its proportions and style, seems to take its place as a link between pagan and mediaeval art. But Nature with its wonderful prodigality spreads its green foliage impartially on either style, binding them together regardless of the difference in age and feeling.

The mediaeval cathedral with its majestic façade, painted by Time with lovely browns and greys, stands upon a broad square at the top of a great flight of steps and faces the main road that descends to Terracina Nuova.

The interior of the cathedral is imposing, and it would be still more so if the eye were not disturbed by some commonplace, so-called artistic, additions of the periods of decadence. We stood admiring a most beautiful *Cosmatesque* marble pulpit of the twelfth century, with fine carvings and inlaid mosaic, supported on twisted columns. And while we thus stood our attention was taken by an elderly woman with lovely Roman profile and dark eyes, kneeling on the floor with her arms stretched out in a most fervent attitude of supplication. It seemed almost as if she were imploring mercy from a judge who had condemned her only child to death. Her sorrowful expression was indeed as intense as that depicted upon the mother of the

Maccabees kneeling by the bodies of her seven
murdered sons, or a Madonna at the foot of the
Cross by a Mantegna, a Crivelli, or a Memling.

We approached gently without being noticed
and discovered her to be praying before a life-size
carved and painted crucifix in a glass case. It
hung upon the wall and was surrounded by
thousands of votive plaques of silver. Models in
that metal of arms, legs, hearts, and so forth,
testified to graces received by many of the faithful
who had knelt there seeking them.

The real hair of the crucifix, hanging from its
bleeding head, those realistic eyes and tears of
glass, the tricklets of blood issuing from every inch
of the torn body, the wounds in the hands, so
terribly elongated by the dead weight, the deathly
white of the flesh covered with livid patches caused
by the falls and blows,—to our eyes all this realism
was unpleasant. It failed to stir in our hearts the
same tumult of compassion that it undoubtedly
did in that of this woman. The head of a dying
Christ by a Donatello would doubtless have left
her unmoved. Her sorrow seemed so great and
sincere that we could not help wondering whether,
after all, such expression in what can only be
considered a low grade of art, was not equally
good, or even better, to raise emotions in certain
hearts than what we know as high art.

We went round the whole church admiring the
many beautiful things it contains, and, when we

left, the woman was still there on her knees praying as fervently as ever.

The most beautiful subjects for painting were discovered everywhere in the town. One could spend years in recording them without exhausting their possibilities. But I had to limit my enthusiasm to making a few paintings, one of which was that of the mediaeval shop in Via Mattonata. I selected this subject because it was so full of colour, and also because the house next door has a romantic history.

Above the Gothic green door will be noticed a small window, through which in the days of long ago must have appeared half concealed on many occasions the strong head of a man who may be called the Robin Hood of Terracina.

The story of the origin of this romantic character, and of his ultimate fate, is not very clear. But what *is* beyond doubt is his reputation for a wonderful career of highway robbery and his philanthropic deeds. Nowhere is it suggested that he gave to the poor every penny he " earned " after allowing for " running expenses ", but it is certain that for years he maintained a large part of the poor population of Terracina entirely with money taken from the rich.

It is said that his strategy was equal to that of a Buonaparte, his courage to that of a lion, and his charity to that of a saint. It would seem that he had several comrades who spread false reports of his whereabouts, to mislead the soldiery. Thus on one occasion on the same day he was definitely reported to have been seen walking in the Corso in Rome and at Chiaia in Naples.

As a matter of fact both rich and poor helped him to escape punishment—the rich for fear of revenge,—the poor for fear of losing what they must have looked upon as a regular income.

After spending five most pleasant days in painting and seeing the sights, and without fear of being robbed on the way by Terracina's Robin Hood, we returned to the town of the Caesars with an unabated wish to see every one of the artistic jewels that make so worthy a diadem around her fair forehead.

MEDIAEVAL SHOP IN VIA MATTONATA, TERRACINA (page 125)

CHAPTER XIV

ROME, HADRIAN'S VILLA, TIVOLI AND SUBIACO

ON a Monday we started early by motor on a memorable excursion of several days' duration. Our idea was to include those three notable places, the Villa Adriana, Tivoli and Subiaco. But soon after passing the St. Lawrence Gate another place of much greater interest came under our notice. This was St. Lawrence Outside-the-Gates. We stopped there and were indeed glad that we did so.

It had always been the custom of the early Christians to build a church above the tomb of a great martyr buried in the catacombs below. So the basilica of St. Lawrence was built over the resting-place of the body of that saint. Commenced by Constantine in A.D. 380, it still stands over the catacomb of St. Cyriaca. The church is one of the finer examples of Christian architecture.

Constantine's original building forms the sanctuary of the present building, the nave of which was added at a later period, and contains all the

features of a romanesque church. The marble
episcopal chair, the pulpit and the floor are
decorated with beautiful mosaics. The side walls
of the nave, supported by twenty-two columns of
oriental granite, are resplendent with modern
frescoes by Fracassini, Grandi and Mariani, one
of which represents the stoning of St. Stephen, the
first martyr.

Under the High Altar are kept the bodies of St.
Lawrence, St. Stephen and St. Justin, and in the
crypt is also to be seen the slab on which the body
of St. Lawrence was laid after his ordeal by fire.
The stone still bears marks left by the burning of
the body.

The modern mosaics and marble decorations
of the crypt, where, after a midnight journey
through the streets of Rome, the venerable body of
Pius IX. was laid, are the gems of the place. The
simplicity and refinement of the marble carvings on
the walls and the design of the sarcophagus are
well in keeping with the church and the simplicity
of that Pope. I still remember the ceremony of
the kissing of his foot, as he lay in state in St.
Peter's, and the terrible crush to get to the church.
Great disorder had been predicted, but, after all,
nothing serious happened.

In about an hour after crossing the Campagna
we reached Hadrian's Villa, which stands on one side
of the old Via Tiburtina, on the very slopes of
Tivoli. Even to-day there are to be seen here the

remains of baths, libraries, temples, museums—
all things that had been the fruit of impressions
gained by Hadrian in his lengthy travels around
his empire.

The more valuable statuary and bronzes were
removed by Pius IX. and are now to be seen in the
Vatican and Lateran museums. But those walls,
so beautifully coloured with frescoes, and those no
less wonderfully ornamented by the brush of Nature,
with her deep green mosses and shiny ivy are still
there—the latter covering with greenery the terrible
wounds inflicted upon those walls by Totila the
Goth, one of the greatest vandals among men.

A great admirer of the beautiful, Pope Pius II.,
in the early fifteenth century, once described this
villa in the following memorable words : " Very
near Tivoli Hadrian built a magnificent villa of the
size of a village. The temples, with their great
roofs are still there ; the peristyles, with their
marble columns and porticoes, can still be admired.
And there yet remain the fountains and the baths
kept cool in the summer heat by the waters of the
Arcis. But age transforms all things. At this day
ivy hangs from those walls, once decorated with
paintings or draperies woven with gold. Thorns
and bramble now grow on those seats and snakes
live in the chambers of queens. Thus perishes all
that is mortal."

How wonderful is the avenue of old cypresses
which leads to the Odeum, or Music Hall, and that

to the Nymphaeum, once supplied with fresh water
from above. The Imperial palaces, the temples
of Diana and Venus, Castor and Pollux, the Latin
Theatre, the Lyceum, are all relics of what once
must have been an assemblage of all that was
highest in Greek and Roman taste.

Close to the last-mentioned temple are the dark
and mysterious passages of the Tartarus or pagan
Hell, which eventually led to the Elysian Fields,
where, according to the old mythology, the souls
of the good were to spend eternity in great and
innocent pleasures—where the body lost its weight,
the eyes never closed, and light never abated.
The miniature canal, imitating that which connects
Alexandria with Canopus, has survived in part and
seems almost childish. But at the same time it is
very expressive.

Hadrian, who began his public career at the age
of fifteen, before becoming Emperor of Rome,
occupied great positions in the Empire ; and
Trajan had for the young tribune, general, and
consul the highest admiration. Soon after Trajan's
death he assumed the purple.

It would seem that Hadrian had a great regard
for Plotina his royal master's wife, and that she
reciprocated. In fact it is said that she concealed
for a time her husband's death in order that she
might forge a testament to make Hadrian the sole
beneficiary and to get time to bribe the troops in
order that they might elect him Emperor.

No other Emperor of the age travelled as
Hadrian did, and amongst his attainments it may
be recorded that he was the greatest walker of
ancient or modern times. Once he made a tour
round the Empire which lasted eight years, and he
did it with his head uncovered. In that tour he
included England, where his visit took him as far
north as the Tyne. To this day the remains of
Hadrian's wall, which was built to protect the
Roman province from the Caledonians, are still to
be seen.

It is not recorded whether, even while in the
north, he insisted upon keeping his head uncovered, whether he may not have been the inspirer
of the Blue-coat boys practice of wearing no hats,
or whether his death (which occurred at Baiae
near Naples) was due to a neglected cold caught
in England.

How incongruous is the mind of man ! The
most sacred names of people and places are often
given to things one would never associate with
those whose names they bear. How the name of
the Tivoli of Tiberius, which was ever the abode of
the greatest minds of Rome, and less than half a
century ago was so closely associated with the
celebrated Liszt (who lived at Villa d'Este), could
ever have been appropriated for a music-hall or
cinema is simply amazing. Nothing could be more
inappropriate,—it is enough to make Tiberius turn
in his grave.

From Hadrian's Villa we found ourselves in a few minutes right in Tivoli. According to the ever-critical Romans of the last century it is and has always been a town of bad omen. So much so indeed that up to a few years ago there was a common saying that at

> Tivoli del buon conforto
> Piove, tira vento
> O suona a morto,

which translated means " The comfortable Tivoli, where, if it doesn't rain or blow, the bells toll for a funeral " !

The fact that Tivoli and its surroundings was, to the Roman of old, as attractive as the Alban hills, is enough to show that the saying must have been invented by some latter-day Roman who did not perhaps find the Sabine wines of Tivoli to his taste. As a matter of fact to-day Tivoli is one of the most frequented resorts of Rome.

A part of the old town rests almost upon the rim of a perpendicular rock on which also stands a charming little temple to Vesta and another to The Sibilla. Both are gems of architecture and are situated in most picturesque surroundings. At the foot of the rock, which is one of the features of Tivoli, we visited another most poetic spot,—the grottoes of Neptune and The Sibilla. No pen could better describe their classic beauty than that of Horace, who spent a great part of his life on his secluded farm close to Tivoli, and there wrote most of his immortal verses.

The white waters of the Anio, hurled down the precipitous green cliffs, render the spot one of incomparable beauty.

While admiring the temple of Sybil we were horrified to hear of Lord Bristol's barbarous design to carry the whole temple to his estate in Norfolk. His attempt to dismantle the temple was frustrated almost too late, for only ten columns were left standing.

With a sudden jump we passed to another period of romanticism, that of the Villa d'Este of the seventeenth century. It is celebrated for its pictorial beauty, and, as before mentioned, for its close association with Liszt. It was under that avenue of centenarian cypresses that he wrote several of his famous rhapsodies. He could scarcely have found more inspiring surroundings. The sound of waters dropping in gentle melody from fountain to fountain, and the continuous singing of the birds, must have inspired him greatly,—perhaps as much as did that maiden who, in his younger days, had inspired his first glorious rhapsody.

In the midst of the picturesque range of mountains on which Tivoli rests, with its beautiful villas, temples and cascades, and just about forty miles from Rome, the Teverone (a tributary of the Tiber) starts its picturesque course towards the city. From these heights amongst rocks and crevasses its

rushing stream forces its way to the green plains of
the Roman Campagna and after thousands of
graceful curves meets the Tiber's yellow waters.
But at one time the stream was interrupted just a
few miles from Subiaco, before reaching the plains
of the Campagna ; by order of Nero enormous
dams were thrown across its course to form a series
of lakes overflowing one into the other.

The white marbles of the splendid villas, that
with their caryatides and pergolas surrounded these
lakes, reflecting as clearly as did the image of
Psyche in the limpid waters, are now no more.
Here Nero gave the most sumptuous *festae*, when, in
summer, he removed thither with his court, his
numerous slaves and the hundred asses which
provided milk for the morning bath of his beloved
Poppea !

No conception of man could surpass the magnificence of those gorgeous gatherings, their refined
elegance or their vice and corruption. But time
alters and reforms. The dams have disappeared,
the houses with their triclinium, the temples with
their white columns, the caryatides with their
insidious smiles, the oleanders, the myrtle, all these
have gone for ever.

Some of the galleys, once filled with the elite
and corrupt society of Rome, are still at the bottom
of the waters, crushed by the stones rolled down
from the surrounding mountains. To-day only a
few vestiges of Roman walls remain to mark the

spot where the greatest tyrant of Rome beguiled the hot days of summer in luxury and sensuous ease.

A few centuries later, in the year A.D. 480, a boy was born into the family of a well-to-do man of Norcia called Eutropius. At an early age he was sent to Rome to be educated. He was called Benedict, and it was he who, in years to come, became the great St. Benedict, Abbot, Patriarch of the Western Monks and founder of the first and most renowned monastic order in the world.

At the age of fifteen the fear of being contaminated by his corrupt schoolfellows and the society he had to frequent became so great in him that, forgetting the tender feeling of his parents and the comforts of home life, he escaped from home and betook himself to one of the most secluded parts of the Province of Rome—the mountains of Sublacum.

His devoted nurse, Cyrilla, would not let him go alone, but followed him in spite of his strong opposition and the perils of the journey. At Afidum, to-day Affile, he succeeded in persuading her to return to Rome. Free of the last impediment he left the main road and climbing the rocks, advanced by almost inaccessible ways to the most solitary spot on the mountains. Here he came across some caves, one of which he selected for his habitation. It is now called the Holy Grotto, and from here once could be witnessed the orgies of Nero and his friends.

During his wanderings in search of food Benedict

met with a certain monk called Romanus, who from the rocks above the grotto, used to send down a portion of his bread and vegetables attached to a rope. To this rope a bell was hung which gave Benedict notice of the advent of his scanty meal.

In spite of having, as he thought, left behind all the temptations of the world, and in spite of his constant penance, he was at times terribly tempted by the Evil One. It is recorded that on one occasion the image of a beautiful woman he had seen in Rome tormented his mind so much that he was almost upon the point of returning to the city. During these great trials he threw himself among the briars and nettles at the entrance to his cave so as to chastise his body and gain deliverance.

Tradition says that, in the thirteenth century, St. Francis of Assisi, on the occasion of a pilgrimage to the grotto, grafted a rose on one of the briars, and the next morning the whole field was transformed into a mass of beautiful scented roses. The leaves of some of the roses of to-day bear a sort of variegated mark resembling a little snake which is alleged to give support to belief in the miracle.

As the fame of Benedict's sanctity spread abroad, his life became a model to a great many religious communities, each of which did its best to persuade the saint to join them. He was eventually persuaded to join the monks of Vicovaro, of which community he became Abbot. But finding their mode of living so different from that which he

SACRO SPECO WITH ROSETO—APSE OF THE LOWERMOST CHAPEL,
SUBIACO (page 138)

desired, he soon returned to the Holy Grotto and remained there until he finally left to settle at Monte Cassino in the province of Naples. At the latter place he established the first monastic order of Christianity.

His fame for sanctity became greater every day. So much so that when Belisarius had to return to Constantinople, Attila, the barbarous king of the Goths (who once conquered Italy, bringing destruction to life and art wherever he passed), on hearing of the saint wished to see him. When they met, the king threw himself at the feet of Benedict and remained so until the saint raised him up saying, " You do a great deal of harm and you will do more : you will take Rome, you will cross the sea and reign nine years longer ; but death will overtake you in the tenth, when you shall be arraigned before a just God to render an account of your conduct ". Great was Attila's terror on hearing this prediction, and from that day he became more humane in dealing with his prisoners.

From Subiaco, by an ever-rising picturesque path one comes to the walls of the Sacro Speco, or Holy Grotto, and here every stone and tree tells a story of great interest. Legend says that the old olive trees we see, so strangely bent towards the pathway, bowed in veneration to the saint as he passed and so have ever since remained.

At the top of this very steep way one also comes to the very top of the sanctuary which is composed

18

of a series of chapels connected one with the other,
all resting against the perpendicular rock and
covering the grottoes. The exterior of the lowermost
chapel is seen in the illustration as also is the field,
once of briars, now a garden of roses.

It would be difficult to establish with precision
the date of these buildings. But one is not far
wrong in attributing some of them to the fifth or
sixth century. Once the entrance was at the lowest
of the chapels, close to the roses, and pilgrims used
to ascend the irregular steps upon their knees.
Now the entry is from above.

The chapels are decorated with wonderful
frescoes representing the life and miracles of the
saint, painted undoubtedly by the monks themselves. The monks in those days were the architects, builders and decorators as well as illustrators
and painters of manuscripts. As proof of their
artistic ability it would be sufficient to examine the
codices and bibles in the famous library of the
Church of S. Scolastica, built on the slope of the
same mountain as the Sacro Speco. These
manuscripts are rare examples of illumination.
It was in this monastery that the art of printing was
first started in Italy.

If the artists who painted those frescoes and
illuminated those books were great, a greater artist
still has been at work upon the stones themselves.
Their wonderful tone may be due to the iron con-
tained in them or perhaps to something in the

THE MADONNA OF PIETRA SPREGATA, SUBIACO (page 140)

THE GATE OF THE VALLEY, AFFILE (page 144)

thundered from all sides. A veritable sea of hands held up glasses of red wine, and all drank to the health of Affile's great hero. The girls who could not embrace him, embraced his wife or equally handsome sisters instead.

The turmoil was soon still more increased by the deafening fire of *mortaletti* (mortars) fired off, without much warning, right behind the backs of the crowd. Rockets innumerable and of all colours, but chiefly of the patriotic white, red and green, soared aloft and spread fantastic lights on the happy faces below.

From the top of a tall house was lowered a large bundle which, when unfolded, proved to be a paper balloon. The hot air from some burning straw inflated it to a great size and, when nearly bursting, a large sponge soaked in petroleum was lighted beneath it and finally it was set free. A clever twist as it rose exposed to the view of the crowd the words " Viva Graziani ", painted in great black letters. Thus metaphorically the General ascended to a great altitude amidst a final burst of genuine and enthusiastic applause.

Affile is a delightful mediæval town of a few thousand inhabitants. It is built upon the rocky mountain-side so that only the Piazza with the church and a few adjacent roads are upon the level. All the remainder is at a slope of forty-five degrees.

The Colle Meridiano, the Regent Street of Affile, is nothing but an interminable flight of steps thickly populated with donkeys, some scrambling up and others sliding down, with cumbersome bundles of hay, wood, straw and all manner of baggage upon their backs. When two of them, recognising each other, stop to have a friendly chat (so to speak), all the traffic of the Corso stops also. Only the sight of the big stick carried by their drivers will induce those intimate friends to say good-bye to each other.

My painting of the Gate of the Valley will give you a good idea of the picturesqueness of that street. I started painting it early in the morning, but the traffic became too great even for an artist. In fact one of those donkeys, in coming down the steps at a speed that he clearly never intended, with a voluminous cargo of furniture on his back, caught my easel with the leg of a large kitchen table and, before I could move, painting and all disappeared amongst a disorderly crowd of quadrupeds. With a courageous effort I plunged into their midst, dodged several other cargoes coming in opposite directions, and eventually recovered my property. My next sitting, to finish the painting was made at dinner time, when even the donkeys take a siesta.

So small a place as this has reason to be proud of itself. Besides being the birthplace of the hero of Lybia, it was also the birthplace of the first

MEDIAEVAL HOUSES, ALATRI (page 145)

church organ. It was in one of those little streets that the original instrument was built, in the sixteenth century, by a man named Spadari. His descendants are still there carrying on the same trade.

From this delightful little place we motored to Alatri, passing through very mountainous country with most picturesque villages perched on apparently inaccessible peaks, where men and women of the purest Greco-Roman type are to be seen. Known as the Cioiari, these people find themselves in great demand as artists' models, both for the classical beauty of their features and for their picturesque costumes. They flock to Rome, where the Piazza di Spagna is their chief rendezvous. Alatri was once the greatest stronghold of prehistoric races. The Cyclopean Walls make an impregnable citadel on the top of the hill, and are the biggest and best preserved in Italy. Almost touching these walls you see the mediaeval Alatri built on the slope. The illustration of one of these streets with its little shrine in vivid colours is typical of the town.

CHAPTER XVI

BEN HUR

On our way back to Rome we had the happy inspiration of entering the city by a different gate—that of the Porta Maggiore, as in crossing the Campagna to get on to the other main road, at a few miles from Rome, we found ourselves in front of a large group of imposing old buildings, like a great town, surrounded by high walls like those of Jerusalem. What surprised us still more was the great animation of the people who thronged the streets.

We were upon the point of looking at our map to discover what place it might be when, to our amazement, we were told by a bystander that it was the newly erected setting for the production of the now well-known American film "Ben Hur".

We sent in our cards to the producer, a typical American in shirt-sleeves, knickerbockers, a big cigar and large spectacles. We were received with the greatest affability. One of the many guides, ready to take visitors about, was put at our service,

146

and in a couple of hours we inspected all that huge installation.

The perfect organisation and the speed at which a film taken only a few minutes before was developed and projected on a screen, to decide if it were good enough, brought to my mind a visit I once paid to one of the seven wonders of America—the slaughter-house of Chicago—very different indeed in character from the Tivoli and its surroundings. At Chicago I had watched, with a properly appointed guide in full uniform (as if he were a custodian of the British Museum or the Uffizi), how a live pig could, as the guide said, descend from the top-floor, where we had been taken, more quickly than we could ourselves. In fact, when we reached the ground-floor that pig had been killed, skinned, boiled, minced and turned into something like a hundred feet of sausages !

This American film company appeared to have hired for some years a large portion of the Roman Campagna, where a faithful life-size representation of an ancient town had been carried out with amazing fidelity. A Roman triclinium, a large swimming-bath, a Jewish town with its cobbled roads, the ancient walls of Jerusalem with one of its massive gates, were amongst the many buildings to be seen.

The most important, however, was the Circus Maximus where Ben Hur was to run at the great race, his chariot drawn by four magnificent white horses. That enormous circus, seemingly decorated with costly marbles and bronzes, was crammed with thousands of spectators. Amongst them were to be seen the vestals and the Emperor with his court.

The race was almost as exciting as a real one, for no one knew exactly what was going to happen, more especially at one point where one of the *bigas*, or chariots, was to turn over in front of the Emperor —one of the principal episodes of the film.

At another place we saw in the atrium of a Roman house a litter with a semi-nude queen, surrounded by senators, patricians and slaves, the latter fanning her with enormous peacock-feather fans. The triclinium was full of recumbent matrons and youthful patricians feasting and acclaiming.

Under the gates of Jerusalem we saw an incessant procession of camels with their picturesque drivers, going to and from the market, followed by flocks of sheep, women carrying their children, Roman soldiers and beggars. At the corner of the market-place, animated by a dense oriental crowd, Ben Hur, the protagonist of the play, a youth of twenty, one of the most perfect human figures I have ever seen, was anxiously looking amongst the crowd for one who was dear to him.

While he advances the several cameras fixed on trolleys retreat at an even pace. Hundreds of great parabolic reflectors, mounted on lorries, each producing its own current, follow and throw upon the figures torrents of white electric light, even

terraces of their houses, washed by the blue waters of the bay.

Everything seems to conspire against your energy. And at certain moments you begin also to feel as the Neapolitans feel—negligent of your appearance, negligent of everything that surrounds you. All you want is to live, to stretch yourself upon the sea-shore, watch the depth of sky, as blue as lapis lazuli, and the waves breaking so gently upon the smooth sand of the bay. Byron in *Childe Harold* describes the approach to Naples by sea as no other poet could ; yet he is so far behind the real thing. You must indeed go there if you would really understand what beauty is, what colour, what real life means !

The environment is such that people live in the simplest ways—more especially the lower classes. A pair of old trousers to wear, a loaf of bread to eat, and a patch of dry sand to sleep on in the shade of some rock is all they want. Everything else is luxury,—an impediment to the real enjoyment of life.

A friend of mine told me of an episode which exemplifies the philosophy of the race—one that would make you think that they are a nation of Socrates or Platos. On his arrival from Rome he wished to go to an hotel situated in front of the railway station. He did not think it worth while taking a cab, and therefore he approached a young strongly-built man stretched upon the pavement basking in the sun, and asked him if he would care to earn two lire by taking his little bag across the road. Any other man at any other station on the Continent would have jumped at the opportunity of earning so easily a sum which then meant nearly two shillings. Instead, this Neapolitan, moving his head in a majestic negative, said, " Tengo mangiato "—I have eaten. He meant that he did not want any more money for food that day, as he had already all he required for dinner, and until his stomach called for more he would not work again.

Compare such a beggar with the thousands who cannot find sufficient rest for the mania of accumulating more wealth than they really need, and say who is the greater philosopher—the wealthy man in his palace or that beggar in the street.

Naples rests on the sunny shores of its beautiful bay within a vast amphitheatre—its thousands of bright-coloured houses starting so near the blue waters of the sea that the spray kisses with charming impartiality both the young visitor still in bed in one of the comfortable hotels close to the shore and the brown face of the fisherman in his humble habitation.

After a gentle declivity the city begins to climb the rising ground along the bay, and on the right, as we face the sea, the houses seem almost as if piled one on top of another. All are artistically

intermingled with most refreshing gardens planted
with pines and flaming oleanders. This was the
Vomero of which we had heard so much, and from
this vantage point we understood still better that
old saying, "Vedi Napoli e poi mori".

Here we sat for hours at a table beneath the
shady pergola of a restaurant, calmly enjoying this
fresh burst of Nature's splendour. It would scarcely
be an exaggeration to say that we were in a state of
entrancement, from which we were rudely awakened
by a pressing waiter. With an extraordinarily
sonorous "Signori è pronto" he placed before us
two large plates of macaroni and a bottle of
Salerno wine. And there, to the accompaniment
of a charming girl vocalist singing "Funiculì—
funiculà", we spent two unforgettable hours in
profound admiration of that great display of God's
handiwork.

Only from this height can we realise the full
glory of the Bay of Naples. To the right, from the
translucent waters of the bay spring up, like opals
resplendent in the sun, the islands of Nisida,
Procida and Ischia. Farther off Capri, Sorrento,
Castellamare, Pompeii and Portici. In the distance, like an apparition, rises the classic outline
of Vesuvius, always smoking to remind the visitor
that if he waits long enough he may have the
satisfaction of seeing a display of fireworks somewhat different from those at the Crystal Palace.

As a foreground to this overwhelming display

20

of natural beauty stands the harbour, full of large boats of all nationalities, more especially British. The constant movement of these and of smaller craft, with their coloured sails bulging in the breeze, lends animation to a scene resembling to some extent parts of the port of London.

But great as is the animation on the water, infinitely greater is that of the city itself. In Naples there is no night. When the sun goes down the glare of electric lights shine from every shop, restaurant and public place, to be extinguished only when the sun rises again. And this feverish animation is not restricted to the main streets, but is usual everywhere, both in the richer and poorer quarters of the city. Almost every other shop seems to be a café, a restaurant or a place of refreshment.

The roofs of the houses, which are flat, are all converted into roof-gardens, some with pergolas, and others less pretentious with tents, but all resorted to by the tenants and their friends for the benefit of the fine sea breezes.

One could almost say that who is not on the roof is in the street or at a window. The latter is furnished with an iron balcony of elegant design, allowing one to see right through. It is from these balconies, so close to each other and only a few yards distant from the house opposite, that an uninterrupted parley is kept up by the gentler sex day and night.

Lines of linen of every conceivable colour and description hang across the roads from house to house to dry and lend an extraordinary air of gaiety to the scene. The thoroughfares swarm with people of all conditions; crowds of buyers and sellers in a brilliant variety of costumes mingling with donkeys, carts and tram-cars, and all carrying out their work with frantic gestures. The ears are stunned by their cries, the noise of the cart-wheels on the cobble-stones and the cracking of the drivers' whips.

If this medley of sights and sounds seems to us astonishing, very much more so is the midnight festivity at Piedi Grotta, near Posilipo, which is held annually, and at which the public has to decide which is to be the popular air of the ensuing year.

Each competitor brings his own band, and by this emphatic means he publicly produces his composition. The winner is not always the best; very often it is that which by the loudest playing succeeds in drowning the others. The following morning the winning air is "the rage"—it is sung and whistled by every urchin of the street, it is played by the most exclusive bands, and is sold in every street of Naples. The familiar airs, such as "Santa Lucia", "Funiculì—funiculà", and scores of others, are the result of this open-air musical competition.

Naples was once the capital of the Campagna

Felix. The Romans who so assiduously cultivated the art of enjoying life soon discovered the balsamic qualities of the site. And with the growth of the Empire, Naples grew in splendour and in luxury.

But the city, which was called after Parthenope, the enchanting Siren of the Gulf said to be buried beneath those waters, became, with the Romans, a city of great learning. Eventually it was renamed Neapolis, the New City, and there have been left most valuable traces of their civilisation and artistic refinement.

To Hadrian we are more particularly indebted for the development and culture of Naples. Since his time it has been principally a place of luxurious retreat for Romans of all ages.

Among the many wonders we saw and admired there, the most notable was undoubtedly the National Museum. It might well be compared with that of the Vatican for its wonderful treasures, more particularly for its unique collection of mural paintings, bronzes and other antiques brought to light at Pompeii, Herculaneum, Bosco Reale, Eraclia, and so forth.

Even classic Rome contributed to that priceless treasure house, with world-famous works such as the Farnese Bull from the Baths of Caracalla, the Flora and Farnese Hercules from the same site. From Rome also are the Dead Giant, the Venus Calipuge, the Amazon, the Wounded Gaul and many another.

Of the priceless bronzes we were most impressed by the Narcissus, the Drunken Faun, the Bacchus Omphalus and the Sleeping Faun, all of exquisite form and modelling.

It would be impossible to speak of a fraction of all the wonderful things we saw in Naples. But we must not omit reference to a painting by Velazquez at the Pinacotheca. If I mistake not, it was called Vendemmia, or the Vintage. This picture alone would warrant a special journey to Naples.

Many were the churches we visited, chief of which was that of S. Martino, covered from floor to roof with marbles and rich carving. Notwithstanding its sumptuous display of richness we were left comparatively unmoved, more especially after the refined examples of architecture we had seen in Rome.

While at S. Martino we visited the museum of that name and that of Capo di Monte. In the latter we saw an interesting display of patriotic relics. But the most valuable object to be seen there is undoubtedly the great " Crib " (or stable at Bethlehem), crowded with hundreds of magnificently modelled and painted figures some two feet in height.

A view of the Bay of Naples with Vesuvius in the distance may almost be considered one of its exhibits, for visitors go there expressly to admire it from one particular window.

Even the cathedral of S. Gennaro, the patron of Naples, cannot be considered a good example of architectural taste, although it is very interesting in its way.

After the marvellous display of artistic relics from Pompeii we had seen at the National Museum, we could not resist the desire to go there at once. So we decided to leave Naples for a few days.

Pompeii stands on the very slopes of Vesuvius; and one can only excuse the founders of the town for building it in such close proximity by surmising that, up to that time, the volcano had been dormant. Perhaps the extraordinary fertility of that volcanic land, so ferruginous, and the proximity of the river Sarnus, may have been the great inducement.

In origin it is almost prehistoric. It was inhabited first by the Oscans, the Tyrrhenians, the Pelasgians and the Samnites, from whom the Romans captured it about 310 B.C. From the earliest times it was a most prosperous agrarian settlement, but after the Roman occupation it became a favourite resort of Rome, and there Cicero had one of his many summer palaces.

In the year A.D. 63 a fearful earthquake took place, and very little was left of the town. The inhabitants abandoned it for some time. But in a few years it was rebuilt against the wishes of the Roman Senate. Almost as if the gods sent a punishment for disobedience (as some believed), on the 24th of August in the year A.D. 79, before the town was yet completed, it was again destroyed. This time it proved to be for ever. A dense shower of hot ashes from Vesuvius, which covered the town to the depth of three feet, was the first premonitory symptom which made it possible for many to escape. Successive showers of hot *lapilli* and ashes completely buried the highest buildings of the unfortunate town. Episodes of great parental affection are recorded, and sentries have been found at their posts where they died.

Years after, vineyards and olive groves grew over the site, and later all memory of its existence was lost. In 1592 the great Roman engineer and architect, Domenico Fontana, in laying a conduit, came across some of the remains, but, strangely, no notice was taken of the discovery.

Only in 1748 did actual excavations commence, when a peasant of the locality, in sinking a well, discovered some painted walls and several objects of art.

To-day the greater part of the town is once more open to the light of day, after lying buried for nearly two thousand years.

No archæological discovery ever revealed so intimately the life of any time or place as did this of Pompeii. The catastrophe was too sudden and unexpected to allow of the removal of many art treasures or articles of luxury. The whole town has disclosed to us the most intimate details of the daily life of the times. After nineteen centuries, we once more see something of the splendour of the ancient town. Forums, temples, baths, libraries, palaces with furniture and magnificent wall paintings help us to realise its former glory.

The red colour of those walls, their marbles, their frescoes (actually encaustic) and the cold mosaic floors, form a wonderful contrast with the deep blue of Vesuvius behind. The note thus struck is characteristic and unique.

Innumerable subjects for painting were to be seen at every step, but an excursion to Vesuvius, organised on the spot, prevented me taking any pictorial record of our visit.

The marvellous mountain was too great an attraction to be resisted. We felt we must climb to the very summit. We ascended by the funicular railway to the accompaniment of that familiar air, " Funiculì-funiculà ", played by a small troupe of minstrels. As we progressed slowly up the almost perpendicular mountain side we saw more and more of the marvellous Bay of Naples with its enchanting islands.

Every moment brought us fresh and more extensive views and in less than an hour we reached the very rim of the crater. The minstrels told us not to forget to look for Procida and *Spain*. " What ! " said I, " Can you see Spain from here ? " " Rather ! " they replied, and thereupon the whole troupe started afresh the words of the Italian air:

" De là si vede Procida e la Spagna ed io veggo a te . . . Funiculi-funicula."

All the superlatives in any language could not express one hundredth part of the great splendour of Nature that lay spread out before our eyes. At that great height, and with all that immense revelation of God's unlimited power around, we felt, now abased at our insignificance and now proud to be the possessors of that God-given intelligence which allowed us to appreciate such glory.

Three guides with ropes helped us to reach the crater's edge, but, on account of the wind, blowing the sulphurous fumes towards us, we had to lie flat on the ground to breathe and wait for a favourable interval before looking down into it.

Finally the moment came and, as Virgil guided Dante in the lowest zone of Hell, our guides helped us to look into what can only be described as an inferno.

Great puffs of yellowish-green smoke succeeded one another, thousands of feet high, and accompanied by internal rumblings. On their way aloft they were fantastically broken up by lateral puffs of deep greenish-orange steam which almost at once became white as snow. Thousands of feet above the crater this weird coloured vapour blends and forms a majestic cloud, which little by little disperses into the infinite blue of the sky.

Wishing to see the sunset from that height, my friends descended to a quieter level to wait for evening. Meanwhile, with the help of a guide, I went round to the opposite side of the crater to take a colour impression of those greenish puffs of vapour and their surroundings.

On my way round I felt very thankful that I had not brought my friends with me ; for I had to walk a long way on the very brink of a precipice thousands of feet deep. I was only able to do this by holding tightly to the guide-rope and turning my eyes away in the opposite direction.

On finishing my painting and getting up from what, at that altitude I considered a tolerably comfortable seat on a rock, I found that my mackintosh had stuck to the rock. The heat of my " easy chair " had melted the rubber !

Sunset surpassed our every expectation. When the golden rays of the sun were almost parallel with the calm waters of the bay, gently catching with liquid light Capri, Pompeii, Naples, the classic gardens and other enchanting places, the emotion in our hearts was almost unspeakable. Everything became golden, even the greenish vapour of Vesuvius and its great column of smoke spreading out in golden glory.

The next day we continued our tour. After seeing Salerno with its beautiful bay and Amalfi, whence comes the celebrated champagne of the Romans, we reached Capri. This is another earthly paradise.

From Annacapri, at the very top of the island, you may enjoy a grand view of Vesuvius and the bay, with Naples at the farthest limit of the panorama. Each little baylet round the island, and indeed every place of interest, still bears either a historic or mythological name, surviving from olden times. The only incongruous name among them all is that of the Villa Krupp.

It would seem that Augustus obtained the island, in exchange for another, from the old Neapolitans. But Tiberius made most use of it,— as a summer-holiday resort of base voluptuousness.

I went alone for a day's excursion to the Blue Grotto, for my friends were not good sailors. After about an hour's rowing among the picturesque rocks we reached the entrance.

"Down with your body!" shouted the boatmen, and skilfully judging his time, he dropped into the trough of the oncoming wave, and, with a hair-raising swoop the boat slipped through the low entrance with little to spare of head room.

A second later we were as blue as the grotto itself, the result of the refraction of the light-rays filtering through the waters at the entrance. The blue, violet and indigo being the most refrangible rays of the spectrum, they are practically the only ones that enter. All the others are lost or dispersed in the waters.

Landing on a flat rock at the farther end of the grotto, I ventured to take a colour record of that marvellous wealth of graded blues. While I was doing so the ghostly form of something like a man, all blue, appeared by my side. For a moment I thought it was the ghost of Tiberius or another restless spirit of the past. Not at all! It was a man of flesh and blood—a clerk in a Charing Cross bank, who had made, I learned, a solemn vow not to return to his post without having taken a dip in the waters of the Blue Grotto.

Notwithstanding that I pointed out to him the danger of the attempt, in a few seconds, like a sea-lion at the zoo, he plunged and disappeared amongst the rocks. A moment or so later he reappeared more ghostly than ever. His flesh had gone absolutely purple with cold. While dressing, with teeth chattering so that he could scarcely speak, he said, " My goodness ! It *was* cold ! " Then I knew him for a mortal.

PORTO TRENTAREMI, POSILIPO, NAPLES

for the arts and sciences flourished for nearly three centuries. It became extinct about 1737. With Lorenzo de' Medici, " the Magnificent ", the family reached the zenith of its prosperity.

On our arrival in Florence, finding the weather somewhat hotter than we had anticipated, we settled at a comfortable hotel at Fiesole. This town stands upon one of a semicircle of hills that almost surrounds Florence, and you ascend to it by a frequent service of electric trains. This ease of access makes it a convenient place of residence for visitors.

We sat at dinner on the vine-covered terrace of the hotel and looked out over Florence. The sun had already set, and below on the plain the city of Giotto, Dante and Michael Angelo was enveloped in a mysterious mantle of darkness. Even the black and white sentry-like Campanile seemed to have fallen asleep with all the other wonders of the town.

With the disappearance of the orb of day Nature provided us with another glory of light— myriads of flickering fireflies whose sparkling beauty can almost be compared with the stars of the milky-way. With the galaxies of stars above and innumerable floating stars around us, delightfully intermingled with the lights of San Geminiano, and Florence below, we seemed transported to a very fairyland of beauty.

And there, calling our imagination to our aid

we visualised still other bright stars which, like those in the heavens, will never fade. Amongst these the most brilliant—Cimabue, Giotto, Petrarch, Boccaccio, Guicciardini, Lorenzo de' Medici, Galileo, da Vinci, Cellini, Andrea del Sarto, Amerigo Vespucci, and the two veritable suns, Dante and Michael Angelo,—have made Florence for ever immortal.

As Rome is intimately associated with St. Peter's, so Florence is with Santa Maria del Fiore, with her superb dome and campanile, the most remarkable building in Europe.

Arnolfo de Lapo started it in 1298, and it was afterwards continued by others, being finally completed by Bruneleschi, whose marvellous dome so much inspired Michael Angelo in the creation of St. Peter's dome in Rome.

Equal in beauty is the Campanile, two hundred and ninety-three feet high, decorated with relief representing the progress of civilisation. From its height we obtained a unique view of the town and the beautiful dome just below, and we soon realised why many people prefer the wonder of Florence to Rome. The façade and the bronze doors are modern, but in perfect keeping with the rest. They do much credit to our times.

In front of this new work stands the Baptistry, so renowned for those other doors by Ghilberti, which Michael Angelo, in a burst of enthusiasm, said were worthy to be the gates of Heaven.

Many are the other churches of Florence, and some are of great merit. The Or San Michele is most beautiful, especially its exterior adorned with statues by the most eminent sculptors of the time. It forms, with the Woolmarket and its external shrine, a most beautiful landmark in Florence. I have attempted to reproduce something of the beauty of the latter in the frontispiece of this book, and from this you may form an idea of the general tone of the stones of the city.

The elegance of the two columns and the arch against that background of mellowed walls, is matched by the note of colour given by the coat of arms in stone, carved, painted and gilded, by the little Madonna and Child and by the blue starred ceiling. These give a characteristic note to the whole.

Within this building in olden times the wool merchants displayed their goods for sale. There must have been many of them, for Florence was always of high repute in the wool trade as well as in the marketing of silk and brocades of all descriptions. Splendid examples of these products may be seen in the Bargello and at the Victoria and Albert Museum.

Innumerable are the spots from which the artist might derive inspiration. Little imaginative power is needed to conjure up a mental picture of what those streets must have looked like when animated by crowds of people in their old-time costume. We are helped in the task by memories of the crowds painted by Benozzo Gozzoli.

The Ponte Vecchio, with its shops on each side like old London Bridge and its throngs of shoppers buying ornaments of gold and other precious merchandise, must have been then, as it is to-day, one of the sights of Italy. We can picture Benvenuto Cellini selling the early products of his marvellous genius at the door of his shop, close to the spot where his bronze effigy now stands. Not even his own fervent imagination and pride could have anticipated that some day kings and popes would almost quarrel amongst themselves to obtain specimens of his work.

Florence is filled with the memories of great men. Here you may see Donatello's shop (in his time the term "studio" was unknown), there Dante's house, farther on the birthplace of Michael Angelo. All of these to-day are marked with appropriate marble tablets.

Besides Santa Maria del Fiore there are other churches of great merit. Santa Maria Novella, with its Ghirlandaio frescoes, is a great monument rendered still more wonderful by the brush of this first teacher of Michael Angelo. San Miniato, on Piazza Michael Angelo, is another of the treasures of Florence. From here you see the Piazzale below with the Michael Angelo monument and, still farther down, Florence spreading in all directions almost up to Fiesole. This is another of those views which can never be forgotten—one that inspires wonder at the genius of man.

One afternoon we went to visit what may be called the Pantheon of Arts, Letters and Sciences— the Santa Croce. Here we spent considerable time before the beautiful monuments to Michael Angelo, Dante, Galileo and many others. Towards evening we went to see a much spoken of fourteenth-century chapel lately discovered in a vineyard a few miles away. The owner of the vineyard was an old friend of ours, who gave us permission to look over the chapel.

One of the labourers, a very handsome young man, clad only in a shirt and cotton trousers,— poor enough but immaculate—and with no shoes, opened the gate for us on our arrival. He read the order to view and with a profound bow, holding his large straw hat in his hand, escorted us up the vine-clad hill to the chapel. On the way he gave us a most interesting account of its history and artistic merits.

It seemed that its chief beauty was its frescoes. Repeated layers of whitewash had formed a thick encrustation on the interior walls, but it had in part peeled off, disclosing fresco painting beneath. On the discovery being communicated to the government authorities, experts examined the frescoes, recognised their importance, and the chapel was declared a national monument. It thus passed under the strict surveillance of the authorities. The frescoes are marvellous examples of mural painting by some unknown master of the fourteenth century. We were indeed glad that we went to see them.

Our guide made our visit even more interesting than it would have been—in fact very soon we became more interested in him than in the frescoes. He told us in language worthy of a Petrarch that although his family did not own the vineyard yet his ancestors had lived in the house below in the fourteenth century, and undoubtedly some of them must have watched the artists painting those walls. His estimate of their quality he summed up by saying that " for purity of line and suavity of colouring they could vie with that of heaven ".

Describing with exquisitely turned phrases many of the sunset effects he had seen between those cypresses around the chapel, he remarked, " When the sun casts its last beams of light on my Giotto down there I feel proud indeed to have been born a Florentine."

Before we left he took us to his house to see what he termed " the pride of his family ",—four magnificent repoussé plates of the fourteenth century with names and arms of his ancestors thereon. He almost laughed at my suggestion of acquiring them. " Many offers we have had from museums, but we would prefer to go without boots for Sunday rather than not see any longer our plates above our fireplace." Such is the aristocracy of the working class of Florence.

No attempt should be made to describe what
we saw at the Uffizi Gallery, a notable building by
Vassari.   The treasures there are too numerous for
assimilation in one lifetime.   Not only do you find
the most famous paintings and sculpture of the
Risorgimento but such world-masterpieces as the
Venus de' Medici and the Apollo Niobe with her
three children.   Michael Angelo, Raphael, Titian,
Beato Angelico, Fra Bartolomeo, Leonardo, Botticelli and all the great masters of every school are
largely represented.   Botticelli, of relatively modern
vogue, is to be studied in the Uffizi far better than
in any other gallery in Italy.

We saw art-treasures of amazing beauty both in
the Bargello Palace and the Palazzo Vecchio, the
last of which is surrounded by a striking tower which
dominates the Piazza della Signoria and Florence.
It contains the famous " David " by Michael
Angelo.

It is on this Piazza that we see the arches of the
celebrated Loggia Lanzi, where we admire the
modern group by Fedi and the Rape of Proserpina.
Above all of course is Cellini's masterpiece—the
Perseus—standing so beautifully upon a pedestal
of equal merit, also his work.   While we admired
the beautiful modelling of that figure we could
almost hear the crackling of his wonderful studio
furniture, which in a moment of despair he pushed
into the furnace when he had no more fuel to
complete the fusing of his metal.

23

Art treasures of equal importance are to be seen in the Pitti Palace. Attached to the apartments of the king, the galleries are decorated with stucco and painted ceilings of great merit. The Bobbi gardens of the palace are unique for their beauties, in character resembling somewhat those of the Villa Borghese in Rome. Here you see, amongst the many statues that adorn the walls, the four unfinished marbles by Michael Angelo.

Many of the great masters we have mentioned are better represented in the palaces and churches of Florence than in the galleries. In fact in no gallery did we see such fine works of Benozzo Gozzoli as we did at the Palazzo Riccardi, that superb example of Florentine architecture.

Gozzoli was endowed with a prolific imagination and an amazing power of execution. The chapel painted by him in this palace is one of the greatest treasures of art in the world. Likewise of great artistic value are his frescoes at St. Agostino in San Geminiano and those at the Campo Santo di Pisa.

Beato Angelico and Giotto must also be admired on the walls of churches if their merits are to be fully appreciated. San Marco at Florence, now a national museum, is full of Beato Angelico's frescoes, and from their pure beauty you gather something of the ecstasy of soul with which the painter worked—often on his knees in the act of prayer. It was due to this almost super-normal state of mind that he never retouched his work.

Giotto, soon after he had been taken by Cimabue into his house as a pupil, surpassed his master and produced frescoes of incomparable greatness. Although those at the Arena Chapel in Padua are the best he ever accomplished, yet when he was summoned to Florence in 1334 he carried out mural decorations for Santa Maria del Fiore which are of the highest value.

Ghirlandaio's most important mural paintings are in the Sassetti Chapel in Santa Trinità. But most interesting of all are those of the choir of Santa Maria Novella, where his young pupil Michael Angelo helped him in his work.

Michael Angelo, the most gigantic genius the world has known, was a great architect, sculptor, painter and engineer. In his mural painting he showed a broadness of treatment and refined sense of beauty such as no other artist before or since has evinced. In Rome we admired him as a divine architect and painter. Here we admire him as a sublime sculptor. With him art was religion; to offend against a right principle of art was for him to offend God himself. As Dante with his *Divine Comedy* influenced the whole world, so did Michael Angelo with his brush, his chisel and his compasses.

His "Pietà" in St. Peter's and his "Moses" in San Pietro in Vincoli, Rome, are masterpieces. But they are not greater than that other burst of his many-sided genius—the Medici tombs of Florence. The " Day " and " Night ", " Dawn " and " Twilight " are works that could only have been carried out by one who looked to immortalise the Creation of God—and for that he was called " Divine ".

Its many associations with the past, its beautiful surroundings have made Florence a favoured and permanent abode of many foreigners, more especially of the English, Italy's truest friends. Queen Victoria and nearly all the crowned heads of Europe at one time or another have had villas there. The colony of English residents is very large and includes many artistic and literary notabilities.

CHAPTER XX

BOLOGNA

WE left "La Bella Firenze" in the morning almost with tears of regret. The things we were leaving behind were far more in our thoughts than the beauty of the scenery through which we travelled.

All too soon we lost in the distance the superb outline of the Duomo of Brunelleschi and the Campanile of Giotto, which the traveller sees first and last in arriving and departing from Florence. When these had faded into the distance, still with our eyes turned in that direction, we gave a last glance to Fiesole.

Our feeling of loss, however, was to some extent tempered by thoughts of what was yet in store for us—the towers of Bologna, the mosaics of Ravenna and the lagunes of Venice.

At the foot of the Appenines in a wonderfully fertile valley rests Bologna, the city that from time immemorial has justly been considered as one of the chief centres of learning, not only of Italy but of the world. For a long time its origin was attributed to the Liguri, the Umbri and the Etruscans ; the latter settled more or less permanently at Bologna, about eight hundred years before Christ. They have left traces of their civilisation.

But, not long since, important discoveries were made, which allow us to attribute the origin of the town with certainty to a very remote prehistoric period.

It was at Bologna, in the fifth century of our era, that the university was founded—the university at which, in the twelfth and thirteenth centuries, the most profound study of Roman Law was made. For us to form an idea of the learning of the city and its world renown, it is sufficient to remember that in those early days the number of students reached five thousand, and later on ten thousand. Its attainments justly earned it the titles "Bononia Alma Mater Studiorum" and "Bologna la Dotta".

Dante, Petrarch, Boccaccio, Tasso, Copernicus and hundreds of other great men have, at various periods, studied at this seat of learning. Galvani, the famous physiologist and anatomist, the discoverer of animal magnetism and electro-deposit (even now known as galvanism), was also Bolognese. So, too, is Guglielmo Marconi, the famous inventor of wireless telegraphy, and so was that marvellous man of the early nineteenth century, Cardinal Mezzofanti. The son of a carpenter this ecclesiastic spoke no less than forty-two languages, besides some sixty dialects. Lord Byron in mentioning him deplored the fact that Mezzofanti was not alive during the building of the Tower of Babel ; had he been there he would certainly have been employed as a general interpreter, and he would have rendered perhaps more extensive service than all Cook's interpreters put together. " I tried him ", Byron says, " in all the tongues of which I knew a single oath and egad ! he astonished me, even to my English."

Few other towns in the world have passed through such political and religious turmoil as Bologna. The best and most pacific period of its life was in the time of John II. of Annibale, under whom it reached the zenith of its artistic, scientific and literary attainments. Unfortunately the invasion of Charles VIII. and the policy of the Borgia shook the whole Italian peninsula, and John with his family eventually passed into complete oblivion.

Another most puissant family, the Bentivoglio, came into power soon after. But their ascendancy did not last long. In the year 1511, after a prolonged and sanguinary dispute, they had to abandon the city for ever. At that period Benedetto XIV., better known than his predecessor, encouraged science, art and literature.

Bologna had always been a town of independent spirit, ever fighting for its liberties. From the nature of the people one would never have dreamed that Bologna would one day have become a stronghold of Fascism.

For many miles before you reach Bologna you see the Asinelli tower, erected by the powerful family of that name, completed in 1105 in the fourth year of its building. It stands as a majestic sentry over the town, as it has stood through the centuries, ready to spit fire or drop stones, liquid lead, hot pitch, and kindred gentle dissuasives, upon the heads of any who should approach with evil intent.

It has a pronounced inclination to one side that is indeed alarming to the visitor—one is almost afraid to pass beneath it. And this leaning from the perpendicular is made more pronounced by the fact that the Garisendi tower, close beside it though only half its height, inclines also, but in an opposite direction. Much has been written about the inclination of these towers. Some think they were expressly built out of the perpendicular, while others say that the foundations have given way under the great weight. At all events the fact remains that in all histories of Bologna the towers are described as leaning.

Many legends are current about these two towers, built nearly a thousand years before any skyscraper of New York. One of these recounts that a member of the Garisendi family asked in marriage the daughter of the Asinelli, who answered that he would consent on condition that the other would build another tower as wonderful as his own. Having done so the two families were united and

" lived happily ever after ".   Another legend attri-
butes the name of the taller tower to a young man,
a dealer in donkeys (*Asino* being the Italian for
donkey), who fell madly in love with a girl whose
father consented to their union if he would build
the tallest tower in Bologna—hence the name
Asinelli, " little donkeys ".

Dante in his *Divine Comedy* has some very beautiful
lines about the Garisendi tower.   At the present
day these may be seen engraved upon a small
tablet at its base.

Besides these two there are the remains of many
other towers in Bologna, though most have now
been incorporated in other buildings and only
traces of them are visible.

In the city there are about three hundred
churches, the majority of which contain pictures
or sculpture of merit.   S. Petronio, the cathedral,
is striking both for its style and size.   But the
church most to be admired is S. Francesco, dating
from the twelfth century.   The interior is especially
noted for its many treasures of art, particularly for
the wonderful reredos, the work of Pier Paolo delle
Masegne and a certain Jacobello in the fourteenth
century.

Round the High Altar there are eight chapels,
all decorated with beautiful modern frescoes, wall
carving and painted windows. The decorative
conception of every one of these chapels is indeed
original, and would undoubtedly stand comparison

24

with any old work of the best period.   A delightfully refreshing hour may be spent with those exquisite works of art.

The exterior, especially at the rear, is a symphony of colour, with its two fine sepulchres of the Glossatori, constructed about 1250.   The pointed majolica roofs of these two monuments give such a note of colour that they cannot be forgotten any more than can the soft, rich colouring of the walls in the church itself.   In the reproduction of my picture will be seen something of this richness and beauty.

Santa Maria dei Servi is another of the many marvels of Bologna.   It is especially notable for its front porch, of the fourteenth century, in which purity of line and the tone values laid upon it by the hand of time are quite remarkable.

Beautiful palaces may be counted by the hundred, but without doubt the Palazzo Bevilacqua is one of the best examples of architecture and exterior decoration of the *Risorgimento Italiano*.   The foundations were laid in the year 1477 by a certain Nicola Sanuti, Count of the Porretta, who took great interest in the building.   He died in 1488 and left it to his wife Nicolosa Castellani, who for an unknown reason passed it on to Giovanni Bentivoglio.   It is not certain who the architect was, but it is believed with good reason that he must have been Jacomo Philippo da Ferrara or Benedetto di Michele da Pistoia.   The façade is

TOMBS OF THE GLOSSATORI, CHURCH OF ST. FRANCIS, BOLOGNA (page 186)

character all its own. It is a town of arcades. The fact that you may, in bad weather or in scorching sun, pass almost from any point in the town to another without umbrella or sunshade is entirely due to the interminable arcades that adorn the fronts of shops and houses. It is a feature which immediately impresses the new arrival.

But these arcades are not solely of use to shelter the folk from the rain or sun. They are a meeting-place for the whole population, rich and poor for business or pleasure, for all appointments whether commercial or even clandestine these arcades seem provided. Even in winter they present an ani-mated scene. But in summer during the hot evenings and right into the early hours of the morning they are almost impassable.

There are crowds going one way, crowds going the other, crowds stopping and obstructing move-ment in either direction. All are exceedingly animated; all shouting, all gesticulating in every conceivable fashion.

My friends at first thought that we stood upon the brink of revolution, especially as amongst the crowd gendarmes were to be seen moving with the tide. But it was nothing of the sort. They were all extremely good - natured Bolognese — great speakers, great lawyers, great patriots. That is why they are so animated. They talk to each other almost with the same earnestness that a lawyer would exhibit in his last harangue to the jury on a question of life or death.

One of the greatest inconveniences met by that mass of humanity moving to and fro beneath those arcades is the enormous number of little collapsible tables in front of the restaurants. At the beginning of Spring the proprietors set them out for their customers, and do not remove them until the approach of the following winter.

Sitting at those tables we see all classes of people enjoying macaroni, *cappelletti a la Bolognese*, cool drinks taken through foot-long straws, or ices of varied colouring and flavour.

Here we have a group of gay young men discussing the elegant figure or pretty face of a girl who finds her way intentionally, though politely, obstructed by another group of equally gay young men. To the right there are the papa and mamma with the rest of their family and the nurse, brilliantly dressed and having a great silver comb in her hair, carrying the baby !

To the left is a group of young officers in bright uniforms who are deeply interested in the eye-language of the elder daughter of the family. She, with apparent indifference, fans herself ; but she is not unconscious of the glances given in her direction by a smart young lieutenant of the Savoia regiment.

Unnoticed, but wild with rage and all alone a few chairs behind, sits a young man ready to shoot dead any one who so much as looks at the girl whom

PALAZZO BEVILACQUA, BOLOGNA (page 187)

he thinks belongs to him. This man is " *il codino* ", or " the little tail ", because, as the tail follows the dog so he follows " his girl ", as he calls her, wherever she goes. He has no rights whatever, for he has never ventured to speak to her father for fear of a refusal—or worse. So the young man walks miles and miles, waits for hours and goes home happy or miserable according to the behaviour of the lady.

Undoubtedly the most conspicuous group of all is that of the politicians. You recognise them at a glance. Perhaps the group is composed of a Senator, a couple of Deputies and two Party Leaders —all Bolognese. They all try to talk at once, but one, with a sonorous voice and most persuasive expression of face, strikes a blow with his fist on the table before him. He upsets half the contents of the glasses as it tilts, but he silences his group.

He is unable, however, to silence the unsolicited accompaniment of a troupe of strolling musicians who play with great vigour the finale from " Il Trovatore ".

You hear the *Onorevole* supporting, with all the eloquence and energy at his command, the wonderful work of the Fascisti and the great wisdom of their leader, Benito Mussolini.

As the magic word " Mussolini " is heard by the crowd, they imagine it to be the commencement of a Fascist demonstration. All stand up, and a resounding " Viva il Fascismo, Viva Mussolini " is heard for miles beneath the arcades. The bands of the leading cafés around strike up the "Marcia Reale", mingled with the shouts, " Viva Mussolini, Viva il Re ".

And when they discover it is not a demonstration calm returns.

While there is so much life under the main arcades, there is romance and sometimes drama in the less frequented side-streets. Turning a corner we saw behind a pillar a young man with long hair like a Raphael or a Beethoven, who with a guitar under his arm gazed intently up at a window. He struck a pose and was about to start a serenade when, following the direction of his gaze, we saw a little white hand from behind the venetian blind make a warning motion.

The movement, which would have had little meaning to the passer-by, spoke volumes to the young man. Clouds were in the air—if not indeed a furious storm. With a tragic gesture we saw him throw his cloak over his shoulder, covering his guitar, and with long strides, like an Irving as Hamlet, depart. From his movements and the look upon his face we could sense trouble, and we were not mistaken.

Half an hour later we passed again by the same spot. A great crowd had gathered and gendarmes stood beneath the window. Curious, we also joined the crowd, and to our great amazement we saw that same young man lying upon the pavement,

his guitar still in his hand and his face still looking
up to that window,—by this time deserted. No
doubt it was a case of rivalry, settled on the spot,
instead of troubling the courts.

The feminine element in Bologna is most
beautiful, and this is a fact well known to every
Italian. From the fine lineaments of their features,
their large, dark, intelligent eyes, their graceful
figures, one concludes that they stand among the
most classical types of Italian beauty. In the
case of the women even more than the men, their
Etruscan origin may be recognised. They arrange
their hair exquisitely and yet with simplicity. They
wear their clothes as can few other women. I
would not hesitate to say that the elegance of the
middle-class woman, more especially, can only
find a rival in the Venetian or Turinese.

The art of throwing their large silk shawls round
their shoulders is remarkable ; it must take years
to attain the requisite skill that yet seems so
natural to them all. With a simple movement of
the right arm, up goes the mantilla, or sciallo, over
the left shoulder, to drop at the back in a mass of
elegant folds. It clings to the body without the
least suspicion of vulgarity, but just sufficiently to
hint at an elegant contour.

Only the Romans of old took such a pride in
arranging the folds of their togas, and upon the
perfection of these folds depended much of the
success of their orations. Julius Caesar and Nero

25

spent hours, it is said, in arranging the folds of their raiment before entering the Senate.

Good examples of this art can be seen in any great museum where the draped statues exhibit it to perfection. One would almost imagine that the Bolognese women have been close students of this classic art.

CHAPTER XXI

BYZANTINE ART

A PIERCING cry for help overtopped even the noise
of clashing steel produced by the opposing armies
in conflict at Ponte Milvius outside the gates
of Rome. It was the cry of a drowning man.
The head of a king, still wearing his golden
crown, was rapidly disappearing beneath the
waters of the Tiber. In a few seconds the
grasping hands, holding tightly to the trailing
branch of a tree as a last hope, disappeared as the
last gleam of light was reflected from his golden
crown.

It was the Emperor Massenzio who, with his
army, was thrust into the Tiber by the supernatural
impetus of Constantine's legions, so suddenly
strengthened by the vision in the heavens of a cross
of light surrounded by the words " In hoc signo
vincit ". The last of the pagan emperors was dead,
and with him died all the gods of the forum. The
beautiful and fascinating Venus, the most adored
goddess of the Romans, was hurled from her

pedestal, and in her place was raised the symbol of the Cross.

With the fall of Venus and all the other pagan deities a great change took place in the artistic taste of that age. A new era began—that of Byzantine art. So we may safely say that Art literally died in paganism, to be born again Christian—a re-birth that brought with it all the exuberance of colour and rich imaginativeness of the East.

From the East came the delicacy of the innumerable patterns, the gold and the blue, to replace the simplicity of the cold black and white tesserae or polychrome decoration of the Latins.

No doubt one of the greatest of all those who promoted the new Christian style was Constantine the Great, who, making Byzantium his royal residence, re-named it Constantinople and adorned it with every imaginable splendour of the Orient. But although Constantine promoted and encouraged with all his power the new phase of art, he was not its originator. That glory was due to Greece, and belongs to an earlier period. A great many palaces and churches were built during Constantine's reign, but the art of mosaic reached the highest point only during the reign of the Emperor Justinian, about the year 537, when St. Sofia was built by his orders, the highest artistic talent of the period being employed.

It is therefore to the East that we owe more

decorated by the Cosmati, was almost as great an honour as to possess a precious relic of a saint. The family had the reputation of working more for God than for money, such was the religious feeling they put into every piece of their work.

The Cosmati were not only architects of great repute, colourists as great as Titian, they were marble-carvers such as the mediaeval world had never seen before. And they worked upon their knees as Beato Angelico did before his frescoes. They made the sign of the Cross at the beginning and end of their daily work, and instead of whistling the popular airs of the time they sang hymns of praise to the God for whom they worked. We may see from the archives in the monasteries that they received money, but very probably the settlement of their accounts was sometimes made by promises of masses for the repose of their souls after death.

At the time of great religious zeal in England a king died whose works had been so great and good that all men called him saint. That king was Edward the Confessor. And who could be more worthy than the Cosmati to make the tomb to receive his remains ? Consequently they were invited to London at the time of Henry III., and they must have been greatly pleased to come and work in honour of the saintly king.

They brought with them their stones and their tools, and, after a long and dangerous journey, were received at Westminster by the Abbot. They continued living here and working for several years, and we see from the old records how Richard de Ware, then Abbot of Westminster, visited Rome himself, bringing back rare jaspers and marbles.

CHAPTER XXII

RAVENNA.   VERONA

ON our way to Venice we indulged in another of those sudden decisions which altered so much our original plans for a tour round Italy. We stopped at Ravenna, and were indeed glad we did so.

With the division and decadence of the Roman Empire Ravenna became the seat of the Roman Court. And when Rome was almost forgotten Ravenna was at the height of its splendour. The rich raiment of the court, the rich gifts to the churches, and above all the rich mosaics, were perhaps the most significant evidences of their imagination and taste.

Time has destroyed the glorious apparel, but could not destroy the work in stone, so that we may say with truth that the glory of Byzantine lives even to-day in the Ravennate mosaics.

The origin of Ravenna lies back in the time of the Thessalians or Pelasgians, after which it became Umbrian. Its position on the Adriatic was such that Augustus made it an important naval base.

On the fall of Rome, about A.D. 404, Honorius settled there and created it capital of the Western Empire, and he fortified it against his many enemies.

He did much to embellish it with oriental splendour, but still more was done by his sister, the great Galla Placidia. To her irrepressible zeal we are indebted for the finest churches of that age.

After having passed into the hands of the Goths, Ravenna was recaptured by Justinian, and, later on, after being the capital of the Longobardi, it was captured by Charlemagne and presented to the Church.

The basilica of San Vitale with its baptistry, built by Justinian, is the purest and finest expression of colour ever produced by the hand of man, and it was studied by every master of the Risorgiamento. It was built almost as an imitation of Santa Sofia in Constantinople, and served Charlemagne as a model for his church at Aix la Chapelle. It is teeming with details exhibiting the overwhelming splendour of the East.

We were absolutely astounded when we entered San Vitale. It surpassed our every expectation. All those extensive backgrounds of blue, surrounding saints, emperors and empresses, from whose shoulders fall richly decorated mantles with folds like the flutings of Corinthian columns, studded with gems and decked with patterns, have an exuberance of colour never to be forgotten. In spite of all that strong tone and rich display of detail, all was subordinated to the intended effect. Nothing disturbed the absolute honesty, the suitability of those wall decorations. They were the antithesis of such "decoration" as we see, for example, at the Royal Exchange in London, where pictorial subjects seem to fight and clamour for our notice with a very disturbing effect upon the mind.

This glory of colour, together with that of the other churches of Ravenna, and of San Marco, Venice, are the foundations upon which was built up the colourful glory of the Venetian school of painting. Santa Apollinare in Classe (534–549), takes its stand side by side with St. Mark's and Monreale of Palermo.

Still other memorable feasts of colour were enjoyed in San Giovanni Battista and San Giovanni Evangelista, both of which were founded by Galla Placidia. The tomb of this Empress can only be termed divine. Desirous of taking away with me a record of its unique beauty, and unable to persuade the custodian to leave the doors open or to remain there while I was painting, I was locked in for four consecutive hours. While I indulged in this rich feast of colour my friends deserted me until my release from my voluntary solitary confinement. When I came out my clothes were quite damp from the humid atmosphere of the tomb, but happily I was none the worse.

A notable sight at Ravenna is Dante's memorial in the Church of the Minorites. It was erected by his best friend, the widow Novello da Polenta, with whom he spent his last years of exile, writing his immortal *Divina Commedia*. Who knows what inspirations, in the matter of colour, he received from those mosaics, afterwards to be woven into his *Paradiso*. And while going through the pine forest, whose trees are almost submerged in the waters of the Adriatic, what inspiration may he not have obtained to serve him for " local colour " in his *Inferno* and *Purgatorio*.

As we have noticed elsewhere, Italy has been from immemorial times an enchanted land sought after by all the surrounding states. The province of Verona, like other parts of north Italy, was invaded by the Cenomani in the sixth century before Christ. They settled upon the fertile lower slopes of the Alps, on the banks of the Adige, and there built their capital, Verona.

Once the Roman Empire had become powerful it absorbed the Cenomani, and Verona, with all its lands, became a Roman province. This city gave birth to many great men ; Catullus, Pliny the younger, Vitruvius, and, centuries later, that greatest of all colourists—Paul Veronese. Any one of these names would be sufficient to render a town immortal.

The Etruscans, the Romans, the romantic rulers of the mediaeval ages, and finally the Church, have all left indelible traces of their activities at Verona. The colossal walls and bastions round the city tell us that she sheltered many men of arms. The Roman remains testify to the artistic taste of Verona's best age, the Ducal palaces and monuments to the nobility of her people, and the splendid churches to her religious fervour.

The most important remains to be seen there are undoubtedly those of the Roman amphitheatre, dating from the second century of our era. It is a beautiful example of classic architecture, much smaller than the Colosseum of Rome of course, but in an excellent state of preservation. In fact even at the present day it is used for public performances and sporting events.

The Roman theatre, on the bank of the river Adige, is also most interesting, especially by reason of its situation. From the upper tiers you may enjoy a fine view of the town, its winding river and bridges.

Equally interesting are the bridge and castle of the Scaligeri. In the course of our peregrinations we come across the most splendid palaces and churches, even in the humbler quarters. The romanesque cathedral and the church of S. Zeno, also of the same style, are the most notable. Likewise they are interesting for the exquisite colouring of their old stones and warm brickwork. The doors of S. Zeno are world-famed as examples of mediaeval metal work in low relief.

Near the Piazza dell' Erbe, resembling the Campo di Fiori of Rome, stands a group of imposing buildings once belonging to one of the most notable old families of Italy,—the Scaligeri. For upwards of a century they were the lords of Verona.

Hidden away amongst these imposing palaces you come upon a little square, almost concealed, crowded with beautiful Gothic monuments, all belonging to this old family. The two tombs under those marble pyramids you see in the painting are the Arca di Can Martino and the Arca di Can Signorio. A third tomb, not seen in the picture, is over the main entrance to the church on the right. That is the Arca di Can Grande.

In all our tour round Italy we never came across a more poetical and delightful spot than this. From those equestrian warriors surmounting the monuments one can easily realise that they were lords of the land and a terror to their enemies.

Innumerable are the feats of arms ascribed to the trio ; but those of the Can Grande surpass all others. The mere report that he was saddling his horse was sufficient to cause many of the belligerent barons of the surrounding states to hasten in with offers of unconditional surrender. Can Grande was too much for most of them, though they must have been very powerful, judging by the strength of the bastions and walls of their strongholds. He was here, there and everywhere in battle, the sight of his plumed helmet flying in the distance was sufficient to bring new courage to the heart of his most timid warriors.

TOMBS OF THE SCALIGERI FAMILY, VERONA (page 208)

the aristocratic Turinese,—rich and poor, young and old, became fervent followers of the great Mussolini.

I had been told over and over again that his power of attraction was phenomenal ; and I had begun to think that it was one of those exaggerations that automatically increase by being repeated. Fortunately, however, I had a good opportunity of convincing myself to the contrary.

A few years ago I was asked to be Royal Commissioner of the British section of the International Fine Art Exhibition in Rome. And at the private view I had the honour of taking round this section His Majesty the King, the Prince of Piedmont and the Prime Minister, pointing out particularly those beautiful examples of modern British art I had had the good fortune to secure from among the works of Sir Wm. Orpen, Sir Frank Dicksee, J. S. Sargent, Sir W. Lavery and others, and so on that occasion I had the opportunity of knowing Signor Mussolini. His erect and rather athletic figure, his classic profile, his piercing eye, his spacious forehead, his arched mouth, made me feel as if I were before a Caesar,—a man of old, a great thinker, a man of iron and at the same time a man with a gentle heart ready to do anything for his fellow-countrymen. With good reason he could be termed a lion with the heart of a child.

Thanks to this great man all political parties of Italy to-day are practically non-existent, or submerged. Some have disappeared voluntarily, others by force of argument.

They were parties who were not merely dissenters from the Fascist views, but of a turbulent nature, — always critical, subversive from birth to every principle, good or bad, and always ready to spread discontent in whatever surroundings they might be placed.

Mussolini's famous march to the Eternal City has justly been called the Second Birthday of Rome, and every year its anniversary is kept with much solemnity. Rome on that day was really reborn. All that army of past statesmen who anxiously waited there on that occasion to pick up some bone so to speak, felt uneasy in a new atmosphere. One by one they disappeared, leaving the regenerator a free hand. Abuses of power may have occurred and mistakes may have been committed in that most pacific and bloodless revolution. But after all, what were they compared with the abuses and reprisals in other lands at times of revolution?

To-day Fascism has the full confidence of all the responsible people of Italy, and its army should not be regarded as a mere bodyguard of the King or *il Duce* but as a powerful army of the best Italian blood, always ready to join forces with the sacred principles of love for God, for the King, and for the country. God save Mussolini!

CHAPTER XXIV

VENICE

Could any one ever conceive a more appropriate title for Venice than " Queen of the Adriatic ? " Like a queen in truth she stands there with her fine palaces, her divine St. Mark's, her striking campanile, in the midst of a group of small islands, her golden domes crowning her and her marble feet kissed gently by the translucent waters of the calm lagoon.

Innumerable gondolas and boats with coloured sails pass on, seeming, in their solemnity and composure of movement, like humble suitors approaching the feet of an enchanting queen.

There she stands to-day, still supported on millions of pine pillars imbedded in the sand, as she stood in those proud days of conquest, when the appearance of the Lion of St. Mark on the horizon of the Adriatic or Mediterranean, made Pisa, Genoa or the Mahommedans tremble. The constant attacks of Attila the Hun and other northern enemies soon after her birth drove her to the sea as her only place of safety. There she and her people lived in peace working together like a family for the common weal. And there, thanks to the wisdom of her rulers and the industry of her sons, she became one of the most powerful and intellectual powers of Europe. Her help was sought by every one when danger threatened from those terrors of the sea, the Mahommedans, until finally she placed herself at the head of the greatest flotilla of those times, and, with Andrea Doria in command, destroyed the menace for ever at Lepanto. Had it not been for Venice and Genoa, the power of Mahomet would have spread far beyond Santa Sofia, and the civilisation of Central Europe would have suffered incalculable damage for centuries afterwards.

In Venice everything is different from all other towns ; but the thing you notice first, more especially if you come from London, Paris, or New York, is the perfect silence of the public ways. No horses, no omnibuses, no tramcars, no motors, or motor-cycles, no noisy means of locomotion whatever. The gentle splash of the oars of a gondola, moving along like a stately swan upon a lake, is all the " noise " of traffic there is.

On your arrival you are met by hundreds of gondola " buses " from various hotels ; and, if you have already engaged rooms you soon hear the name of your hotel called out. Your luggage is passed from the railway compartment to the gondola

ANTIQUARIAN SHOP ON THE PONTE DEI DADI, VENICE
(page 223)

and straight away you enjoy your first glide over
the silent waters. Even the oars seldom splash,
they simply cleave their way without a sound.

The enchanting calmness, especially if you arrive
at night, as we did, and with a full moon shining on
the lagoon, gives you at first the impression of being
in a place of sanctity, or at least in some environment of great dignity. Instinctively you speak in a
subdued voice, as if afraid to disturb that wonderful
impression of greatness which envelops you from the
first moment of your arrival.

Gliding over what seemed like a lake of silver
we caught, silhouetted against the moonlit sky,
outlines made so familiar to us by many pictures.
As if old friends we called out " Hello ! Sta. Maria
della Salute ! " " Hello ! Campanile ! " " Hello !
San Marco ! " "We are here at last to see if what
Shakespeare, Byron, Goethe and Browning have
sung is true ! " And we looked around to see if
we might find in other gondolas an Othello with
his Desdemona, a Titian, a Veronese, a Tiepolo,
or a Gian Bellini. All of these had, as if by magic,
become our intimate friends within a few minutes
of our arrival. We felt that they were awaiting
us here ; indeed on the following day they provided
us with a never-to-be-forgotten intellectual feast at
the Accademia.

In a quarter of an hour we were wakened from
our reverie. The gondola touched the step of the
hotel in the Grand Canal. We landed and were

28

soon settled in a comfortable room magnificently frescoed with allegorical subjects.

Continuing our dream, instead of dressing for dinner we sat on the balcony overlooking the canal, until we were called for the third time. An hour later we returned to our rooms, and, in deep silence, sat again on the same balcony where we sunk into a sort of sleep, to awake only in the early hours of the morning. Then to bed to finish our dreaming!

The next morning we had a hurried breakfast as if anxious to catch a train, and at nine-thirty we were again in a gondola. One of my friends, who knew some Italian, shouted to the gondolier, "Presto! Presto! Vogliamo andare da Tiziano!" and, if we had not just emerged from a fine hotel at so early an hour, we should undoubtedly have been taken to some restaurant, or café, named after the famous painter. But I came to the rescue and told the man that we wished to go to see Titian's pictures at the Accademia. He touched his hat and in ten minutes we were revelling in a long anticipated feast of beauty.

A celebrated literary critic, in writing of Dante, said, "Dante is like the sun: it is sufficient for him to show himself." Similarly we may say of Titian and the Venetian school, it is sufficient that they show themselves. One glance around the gallery is enough for their portentous colouring to sink into the remotest recesses of the soul.

There for hours we wandered from room to room; from Titian's "Assumption" to Veronese's "Marriage Feast at Cana",—from Gian Bellini to Giorgione and Tintoretto, each in turn seeming greater than the last. It was a magnificent feast of colour of insurpassable beauty, and in the midst Titian sat as a king with all his royal sons around him.

Great are the works of Titian in Madrid, where he painted for Charles V.; great is Veronese in the National Gallery and the Louvre; and wonderful are all the examples of that school throughout the world. But all fade into insignificance in comparison with the stupendous revelation displayed to our wondering eyes in the Fine Arts Academy, where in strong relief against this background of magnificent old masters emerges another giant in talent,—Gianbattista Tiepolo, who in many ways was greater than Titian. His numerous frescoes which adorn almost every church and palace of Venice, testify to his great reputation amongst his contemporaries. Only gradually, however, has his true greatness begun to dawn upon a learning, modern world.

In Santa Maria Gloriosa dei Frari we saw the tomb of Titian in close proximity to some of his paintings and those of his follower Tintoretto. Amongst the many other churches we visited were San Giovanni e Paolo, with its beautiful stained glass and important monuments of the Doges,

Santissimo Redentore, the finest example of Palladio's architecture, and Santa Maria della Salute, full of historic and artistic records.

San Marco, with its many golden domes and priceless mosaics, stands in majesty upon the most important square of Venice. Close by is the Palazzo Ducale and the Campanile, a faithful copy of the old tower which Galileo, then an old man, used to ascend to make his astronomical observations.

St. Mark's, once a chapel of the Doge's palace, later developed into what it is to-day—one of the grandest expressions of Byzantine art in Italy. Almost every stone in that façade could tell a long story. And if only those four sublime horses of gilded bronze could speak they would certainly boast of being the most travelled horses in the world.

From Greece, where they were most probably made, they went to Constantinople, and with great pomp were brought thence to Venice by Doge Dandolo in 1204. From Venice the rapacious Napoleon took them to Paris, but soon after felt so ashamed that he returned them in 1815. Their latest excursion was to Rome during the Great War, when, for fear of possible damage by aircraft they were temporarily removed to safety. They travelled by a special train after a careful inspection of the line.

How inscrutable is the working of destiny! These horses, soon after peace was declared, re-

turned to Venice without a single scratch upon
their noble bodies ; while the beautiful white horse
of Charles I. of Austria only lately was sold to an
American cinema company never to return to its
native land.

From a majestic atrium with domes decorated
in mosaic of great beauty, you enter into the
presence of an unspeakable glory of colour. Those
five hundred columns of rare marble, those marble
walls and arches all round the church ; above all,
that mass of vaulting resplendent in gold mosaic,
so judiciously broken by figures of angels and
biblical subjects, give to the whole a sense of
majestic beauty that is entirely unique. Monreale
of Palermo alone approaches it.

Besides the fine carvings of the capitals and
bases of the columns, all differing from each other,
hundreds of other details are a source of admiration.
But above all are the two marble pulpits, one on
either side of the screen across the sanctuary.

The mosaic pavements are world-famous, wonderfully in keeping with the whole and yet so varied
and simple both in design and colour. During
our stay in Venice we could not help paying a visit
daily to this church, so great was its fascination.

While there we instinctively compared it with
the great cathedral at Westminster. In the presence
of such a classic example of refined Byzantine
taste as St. Mark's, one felt how much more truly
devotional would Bentley's masterpiece have been

had the interior decoration been designed with a keener appreciation of the ultimate effects of the distractingly strong wave-like " figure " of the cipollino marble.

In the whole of St. Mark's there is no jarring note such as we have at Westminster in the archaic panels of the " Stations ". Figure relief of any kind is almost foreign to the style, and when it is so ultra-modern as to be prehistoric, if not absolutely pagan, it is frankly out of keeping with the simple beauty and high ideals of Byzantine art. One feels that the sacred figure of Christ in a Christian church, such as Westminster Cathedral, allows even less latitude for individualism than, say, the concept of Rima,—a product of the same modern school of thought.

Attached to St. Mark's is the Doge's palace, almost as important a specimen of Venetian Gothic as the church is of Italo-Byzantine. The archway leads to the historic courtyard, with its imposing flight of stairs trodden in ages past by the Doges and the famous Council of Ten. It was here that the unfortunate Doge Marin Faliero passed to his beheading as a reward for trying to save the Republic from the corrupt aristocratic government of the time.

Not content with thus putting him out of the way they even painted his portrait black in the long series of the Doges portraits on the walls of one of the halls of the palace.

The interior is a series of apartments most richly decorated but beautiful and dignified. Here we saw panels and ceilings painted by such masters as Tintoretto, Veronese, and by others of the local school.

Beneath the famous Campanile is the Loggetta, an exquisite piece of fifteenth-century architecture. Close by is the Palazzo Reale ; its Piazzetta, with the two pillars capped by the Lions of Venice is almost washed by the Adriatic.

The picturesque colour of the small canal we illustrate, showing the Arco dei Dadi, with its antique shop perched up on that balcony and the elegant gondola passing under the bridge, is a fair specimen of the beauty of the byways of Venice.

The cloister of San Geronimo, now no longer a cloister, may also give an idea of the colour of the stones of Venice.

The shops, the large baskets of flowers for sale at every corner, the flags on the masts, the multi-coloured shawls of the women, who wear them with amazing art, are all things that contribute largely to render that feast of colour so complete.

Piazza San Marco at night is a veritable ball-room. The military music, the chatter of the animated crowd, the liveliness of the waiters running amongst the tables holding above their heads trays of vari-coloured ices and drinks as bright as flowers, the shining of the moon on the golden domes of St. Mark's, the noise of the hours being struck by two moors who emerge from a niche with large hammers and pound away at the large bell outside,—all these go to make a scene of ceaseless vivacity.

While at Venice we went, of course, to the Lido, the chief bathing resort of the Lagoon. There we enjoyed another beautiful view of the " Queen of the Adriatic ". She looked more enchanting than ever.

On landing at the Lido we saw an animal of which we had almost forgotten the existence ; this was a horse attached to a bus taking passengers to the bathing shore on the other side of the island. In those past weeks in Venice we had completely forgotten horses and motors, and the sight of the first caused a real sensation. I could not help asking the conductor how he got him there, and he, in a surprised and somewhat annoyed tone replied, " In a gondola, of course ".

The Lido is the most fashionable watering-place on the Adriatic, and there you see the best society of all Europe. It is the rendezvous of elegance and frivolity. All the latest fashions and scandals of European society can be seen and heard there. There, too, you may compare under the most favourable circumstances the racial types of America, France and England with those of Italy, Greece, Austria, Spain and the rest. In other words, it is the best summer exhibition of international beauty.

COURTYARD OF SAN GERONIMO, VENICE (page 223)

Fashions in bathing costumes change there as toilet fashions change in Paris. A lady would not be seen enjoying her afternoon dip in the same costume that she wore in the morning. These costumes, the tents and parasols are all of the most vivid colours imaginable and add much to the extraordinary gaiety of the place, so much so that at a distance the sands appear like an immense artist's palette or flower-garden. The effect is quite different from the colouring of a Titian or Tintoretto, yet it is essentially Venetian.

But Venice, with its Lido, is not merely a town visited by foreigners in the bathing season; there are many English people who make the town their permanent abode. The drawing-rooms of the aristocracy are filled with English people, and here too, as in Rome and Florence, the English language is heard everywhere.

Among the public monuments of Venice that we most admired was the statue of Colleoni. There the great rider sits like a proud knight; both he and his horse are of amazing artistic beauty, both in clearness of detail and strength of feeling.

Colleoni of Venice, by Verrocchio and Leopardi, Emmanuel Filiberto of Turin by Marrocchetti, and Marcus Aurelius in Campedoglio, are by far the greatest equestrian monuments of the world. It is a great pity that the artists responsible for the many examples in London did not study these specimens more closely.

29

In our many gondola excursions we passed time and again under the renowned Bridge of Sighs, that of the Rialto and many another fine span.

We visited Murano and all the other places of interest, finding in each some fresh example of beautiful architecture or colour.

Everywhere the animation of the cafés and restaurants adds greatly to the gaity of Murano. The Cavelletto ("The Easel") is the artists' rendezvous, and is one of the most renowned and much frequented by English visitors to Venice.

Even this unforgettable visit eventually came to an end. But before finally saying good-bye to that pictorial lagoon, we visited Padua, where we saw Giotto's great masterpiece, the Arena Chapel, the walls of which are literally covered from floor to roof with exquisite examples of his genius.

We saw the church of St. Anthony, the protector of the town, with its celebrated angel-panels by Donatello. We saw his Gattamelata outside, making a contrast with the warm colour of the church.

The most interesting sight of the town is the Palazzo della Regione, of the eleventh century. The hall is the largest in the world and is entirely decorated with paintings. Here is preserved a remarkable wooden horse by Donatello, the body of which opens like the horse of Troy.

The University is one of the oldest in existence and can boast names among its teachers such as Galileo, Guglielmini and Fallopius, while among its scholars were Dante, Petrarch and Tasso. The town, moreover, was the birthplace of Livy.

The morning after our arrival, we proceeded on our journey to Milan, skirting the blue waters of the Garda Lake, enjoying the fine forms of the mountains behind reflected in its calm waters. Picture-subjects followed one after another as we progressed. Our journey led through vineyards, mulberry plantations and extensive cornfields. Towards evening we obtained our first glimpse of Milan and its Duomo.

CHAPTER XXV

MILAN

In approaching Milan, you feel from the very first that you are coming to something more than an ordinary town. For commerce and industry of every description Milan can justly be called the commercial capital of Italy. On your arrival, the size of the terminus and the imposing square outside the station both confirm your first impression.

As it was our intention to spend several weeks here, we took rooms at a comfortable hotel near the Duomo. From this position we were able to get anywhere in a comparatively short time.

It was already night when we arrived, and crowds of people were returning home by train after their day's work, which does not finish until seven or eight. The bustle reminded us somewhat of the scene at five o'clock at Charing Cross or Victoria. The town was already in a glare of electric light.

While waiting in the foyer of the hotel the

porter accosted me with the voice and gesture of one of the conspirators of St. Bartholomew's night. He told me he could sell us three tickets for the first performance of Boito's opera "Nerone". The temptation was too great to be resisted; having heard so much while in Italy of this great event that was approaching, I accepted the offer without any hesitation, and paid the very high price he asked, and in less than an hour we were seated comfortably in the most celebrated and important opera-house in the world—the Scala of Milan.

We never regretted the rush, nor the price we paid for the tickets. What we saw and heard was too great to allow of any regrets. Musical enthusiasts and critics had arrived from every part of the civilised world, and every ticket had been sold long before. Every lover of music longed to listen to the loudly heralded new opera by Boito, the intimate friend and librettist of Verdi, the author of "Mephistopheles".

The world had been waiting nearly thirty years for the appearance of "Nerone", so the expectation was intense. The boxes were ablaze with diamonds, pearls and flowers. The world-renowned *maestro* Toscanini took his place and raised his baton; the silence was profound as the orchestra began.

After the prelude, a burst of musical genius, the curtain went up. Each succeeding episode seemed greater than the last until we reached the end of

The lateral façades, more beautiful than the front, are richly diversified by four thousand five hundred niches, containing finely carved statues of saints, and by the buttresses which receive the enormous stress of that wonderful roof with such perfect ease and grace.

The vastness of the interior, with its forty-eight octagonal pillars of great size, dividing the whole into five naves and supporting the pointed arches of the roof above, and the four still larger pillars supporting the central lantern, are totally beyond description for their majestic appearance.

Each of the five naves has an octagonal termination or apse in which stand the altars. The latter are all beautiful works of art, as also is the fine iron candlestick, a copy of which is to be seen in the Victoria and Albert Museum.

In the floor, just under the enormous lantern, is a circular opening which has a beautiful marble balustrade and iron grille, through which we can see the last resting-place of St. Charles Borromeo, of the old Milanese family of that name. His work during the terrible pestilence of the sixteenth century was indeed saintly. His great authority kept in submission even the most restless of the barons. But his example and charitable works dominated them more than his ecclesiastical power.

Great as is the impression of the Duomo's beauty gathered from the floor level, still greater is that obtained from the roof. On our arrival there, after

A WING OF THE DUOMO AND THE TOWER OF ST. GOTTARDO,
MILAN (page 233)

understanding with ever-increasing clearness the reason why Browning penned those significant words with which we opened these pages,

> Open my heart and you will see
> Graved inside of it, " Italy " !